Herbert Ypma

111

ADVENTURES

AROUND THE WORLD

THAT  YOU

MUST NOT MISS

emons:

CONTENTS

Foreword

All travel should be an adventure. Life really is too short. So never let an opportunity go by that will create memories … lasting memories.

You have a choice. We all have a choice. You can spend your life collecting things, or you can use your time on this planet to collect memories. Because that's what adventures are. They are memories. And memories are the only things that you can take with you and leave behind.

But please do not think that the only worthwhile adventures belong to faraway places and exotic destinations. Sometimes a memorable adventure can consist of nothing more than a picnic under a bridge. If that picnic happens to be under the legendary Pont Du Gard, on a quiet beach along the river Gard, then it becomes a "monumental" picnic – and a monumental memory.

And money is not of key importance either. There are plenty of adventures in this book that cost nothing or almost nothing at all. The unlikely thrill of a surfing adventure in Hong Kong, for instance, costs no more than a return ticket on the local Metro, a taxi fare to the entrance of a national park and the board rental fee, for a grand total of less than US$60.

Nor do you have to be an adventurer like Bear Grylls, asking yourself, "Will I survive?" There's nothing dangerous, for instance, about taking the night ferry from Naples to the Aeolian island of Salina. But it's definitely a thrill, especially when you witness the famous smoking volcano of Stromboli at dawn from the deck of the ship.

A lot of the adventures documented in this book were not planned. They just happened. And that's part of the charm. A friend suggested visiting a Himalayan monastery at prayer time, and to be honest, it didn't sound that exciting to me. But it's one of the most surprising, entertaining and profound adventures I have ever experienced. So who knew? I certainly didn't.

Upon reflection, I think the most important thing you need for any of these 111 adventures is an open mind.

Herbert Ypma

*All travel
should be an
adventure.*

ON SAFARI

The very word "safari" suggests adventure: something exciting, something Hemingway would like. But a Safari doesn't have to be the exclusive pursuit of big game in Africa. There are many safaris on offer around the world … all very different and all completely unique. What they have in common, whether it's a snorkeling safari in the emerald waters of the Musandam Peninsula, or a romantic skiing safari in the French Alps, is that they all share a sense of the exotic and the spontaneous. In other words, you have no idea what to expect, and that's how it should be. A proper safari is an adventure that should surprise and delight.

walking safari

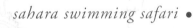

romantic skiing safari •

sahara swimming safari • •oman snorkeling safari

•india tiger safari

maldives surfing safari • •dhoni sailing safari

atacama
horseback safari

•africa walking safari

•

surfing safari

sneak up on a couple of rhinos and a dazzle of zebras!

every safari starts and ends in this rustic 18th farmhouse

1__Africa Walking Safari

The wildlife of the African bush on foot

Trekking through the South African bush on foot is a game changer. Opting to leave the Land Rover behind exposes you to more: more knowledge and more danger. Suddenly, every twitch of a branch or rustle of a leaf gets your heart racing and the adrenaline pumping. But the pure thrill of it is not the best reason to embark on a walking safari in South Africa. It's about what you will learn. It's about discovering the small animals, such as chameleons, as well as the famed Big Five – lions, leopards, rhinos, elephants and Cape buffalo. It's about learning how to read footprints. You can determine the time of day a herd of elephants passed by through looking at the bird prints inside the cavity of the footprint left by the elephants. For example, some birds only walk around at dawn, so if their prints are visible inside the elephant footprint, you know that the elephants passed by during the night. A walking safari in

Africa will connect you to your most basic primordial instincts, ones that you've probably never experienced. Yet in this scenario, they surface quite quickly. It's a dormant part of our evolutionary selves, dating from a time when we were hunting, or being hunted. One thing is certain: you will never again feel as alive as you do whilst walking through the bush. You will discover a part of you that you never knew existed. Your guide is the key. He or she has to have the knowledge and must be a crack with a rifle … just in case. I was lucky enough to embark on a series of walking safaris with the man consistently voted as the best safari guide in Africa year after year. His name is Greg Lederle, and he is the David Attenborough (but much younger) of the Safari world, a big no-nonsense guy, who knows more about the African bush and wildlife than anyone else I've ever met.

___ www.lederlesafaris.com

A walking Safari is all about the small creatures of the African Bush. Being able to pick up a chameleon and watch it change colour, observing footprints of birds in fresh elephant tracks to help determine the time the herd passed by – these are the types of experiences you will have when you venture out into the bush on foot.

2__Oman Snorkeling Safari

Diving in the emerald waters of the Musandam

Many hotels in the world offer snorkeling as an activity. So, what's the big deal? We are talking about a pair of flippers, a face mask and a snorkel. True, the equipment is nothing special – but the experience can be. There is one place I know that has turned snorkeling into a unique and unexpected adventure. It starts with a flight to Dubai. But instead of heading into town after landing, you turn right (Northwest) and head off in your four-wheel drive into the desert. After a brief spell driving across the sands, you end up in the Ru'ūs al Jibāl, the barren, rocky and imposing peaks of the Musandam Peninsula. These are not hills. They are proper mountains, and the road that leads through them winds and twists with the best of them. The journey is both bleak and majestic, and snorkeling is honestly the last thing that comes to mind. Eventually, the road starts to descend steeply towards a big, isolated crescent of sand called Zighy Bay. This is your adventure base. You will get a bungalow built in the style of traditional Omani village houses, probably with your own private pool situated on the edge of the beach. Early the next morning, your day starts with a walk along the beach to the jetty at the far end of the bay, where a traditional *dhow* – albeit a fancy one – is ready to take you to the uninhabited and wild coast of the Musandam Peninsula, in the direction of the infamous Strait of Hormuz. Surrounding peaks plunge dramatically from great heights into the sea, and the water of the Gulf of Oman is so clear and so green that it sparkles a distinctly emerald color. Below, the water is teeming with exotic fish. Having this extraordinary location, dubbed the Norway of Arabia, all to yourself is a privilege you will not soon forget.

www.sixsenses.com/en/resorts/zighy-bay

It's not just the crystal clear, emerald water that defines this remote bay in Oman. The mountains of the Musandam Peninsula are also a unique and unexpected feature, especially being so close to the conveniences of Dubai (an hour and a half journey by car). A nearby peak of these rugged mountains is an ideal and distinctive setting for a memorable and inspiring sunset dinner.

3__Maldives Surfing Safari

Turquoise tubes in paradise

Of all the idyllic destinations in the world, the Maldives must be the most under-estimated and least understood. Sure, it has turquoise waters and white beaches, and of course it's a perfect destination for honeymooners. But with that comes the assumption that there's not much to do except eat, drink, bury your toes in that powdery white sand and dip into the turquoise sea. Nothing could be further from the truth. There's more adventure on offer in the Maldives than in the Caribbean. Few people realize, for instance, that the islands of the Maldives have world-class waves, tall turquoise tubes that break over coral reefs, in the middle of nowhere, with, I might add … no one on them. The swell that rolls through the Maldivian islands is essentially the same swell that feeds the famous surf spots of Indonesia, except here in the Maldives you don't have to share - at least not with very many. There are many breaks, and although there are a few boats that take groups of enthusiastic surfers to a variety of the best surf spots in the Maldives, the options on offer are vast and far apart, so you will probably never see another surfer. I prefer to stay on a beautiful island like Laamu in the southern atolls, in the signature handmade luxury of Six Senses and to take their small rubber boat to Ying Yang, their famous local reef break, to get my daily fix of riding turquoise tubes. This is surfing as you see it in movies and magazines: exciting, breathtakingly beautiful and … empty. Here, you can connect to nature on an almost spiritual level. Just you and the sea, like something out of a Hemingway novel.

_____ www.sixsenses.com/en/resorts/laamu

Turquoise tubes are the attraction of surfing in the Maldives. You motor out past the reefs surrounding the island towards perfect waves booming in the distance. Not only is it a breathtakingly beautiful spot, but you will also likely have it all to yourself. And you have the added plus of heading back to your bungalow situated in a "picture-postcard" perfect lagoon on a beautiful, unspoilt tropical island.

4__Sahara Swimming Safari

Exotic lakes surrounded by sand

The title sounds like an oxymoron. Swimming and the Sahara Desert are the perfect contradiction of one another. And yet, here it is, one of the most unexpected swimming adventures on the planet. It starts with a journey to Siwa - the same ancient date palm oasis deep in the heart of the Egyptian Sahara that attracted Ramses II and Alexander the Great. You stay at Adrere Amellal Eco-Lodge, an extraordinary complex built entirely out of mud and salt on the edge of Siwa's massive lake. It is the brainchild of Dr Mounier Nematalla, an eccentric professor of Ecological Impact Studies at Cairo University. He wanted to prove that style and environmental consciousness can go hand-in-hand very well. There is no electricity here – all the rooms are lit by candlelight, and it's much more romantic this way. Adrere Amellal is an experience in its own right, and it's the perfect base for a Sahara swimming expedition. From here, you drive in a Land Cruiser with the tires deflated into the never-ending dunes of the Sahara. You don't go at a leisurely pace, but rather at breakneck speed so that the tires plane on top of the sand instead of sinking into it. After an hour or so, you get to a point where there are only giant sand dunes in every direction – and a lake, looking convincingly like a mirage, incongruously nestled into the dunes. You might expect that a small lake in the Sahara would be uncomfortably warm like a hot bath, but the water is clear and surprisingly cold. Why? Because it is continually fed by a subterranean lake 100 metres or so beneath the surface. Swimming in cold lakes in the middle of the biggest pile of sand on the planet ... how wonderfully weird is that?

___ www.adrereamellal.com/adrere

5__Romantic Skiing Safari

Crossing borders and exploring unknown pistes on skis

I love to ski, but the repetition of going up and down all day on the same slopes can get monotonous. I much prefer the idea of putting on skis and going out to discover quaint villages, unknown mountains, secret valleys and charming little restaurants I have not eaten at before. There is only one person that I know of in the Alps who offers this kind of adventure. His name is Dorrien Ricardo, the proprietor of an 18th-century farmhouse in the French Haute-Savoie called Le Mas Des Coutettaz, or The Farmhouse. He knows the peaks and valleys of the immense Portes du Soleil ski domain like the back of his hand. Just as importantly, he is a *bon vivant*, a man who loves discovering little goat shacks in spectacular spots that also happen to serve amazing food, and someone who is still as thrilled as the rest of us to find a downhill run that has not been skied before. His skiing safari starts early. By 8am, you will have caught the first of many ski lifts. You will find

yourself in Switzerland a few hours later. Different language, different currency – everyone has to have their passport, just in case. Time for a quick hot chocolate before heading off again, exploring deeper into this, the world's largest linked ski area. By lunchtime, you are back in France at an unlikely hut in the middle of nowhere that happens to serve authentic and delicious cuisine of the Haute-Savoie. By now, if you look at a map, you have covered a mind-boggling distance. To return to the Farmhouse from here by car would take six hours. The afternoon is the morning in reverse: a systematic process of taking lift after lift and skiing slope after slope to get back to where you started. But that's not the end of your adventure. Afterwards, in the evening, there is a candlelit dinner in the old barn of the Farmhouse, an extravagant affair with everyone seated at one massive table – a fitting finale to a most memorable day of skiing.

___ www.thefarmhouse.fr

Every safari starts and ends in this rustic 18th-century farmhouse.

6__Atacama Horseback Safari

Riding in the red valley of death

This place is indeed no country for old men. It's early in the morning on the outskirts of San Pedro de Atacama, a small town in Chile's infamous desert, and it's already quite hot with the sun beating down brutally on this, the driest place on the planet. As you set off, the horses trail a massive cloud of red dust like in a Spaghetti Western. My kids are loving the theatre of it all. The first stage is a gentle trot through town. After leaving San Pedro de Atacama, you start to climb the surrounding hills via steep rocky paths that challenge both the riders and the horses. And then the terrain flattens out somewhat as you approach a steep and narrow canyon, the kind you've seen in those Westerns where someone always gets ambushed. My children were disappointed that we didn't get attacked, but everybody, including the horses, welcomed the brief bit of shade. As you climb even further, you reach strange sand dunes that lie quite unexpectedly between surrounding peaks. They provide an opportunity to go full tilt in a burst of flat-out galloping – which we did until the horses were exhausted. The kids were grinning from ear to ear. My son, who compares everything to *Star Wars*, likened this experience to exploring the planet Tatooine. Next, it was time to rest the horses, to drink and eat, and then we set out to repeat the adventure, in reverse. By the end of the day, there was still time left to dive into the hotel's horizon pool, the movie-style ending to the perfect horseback safari.

www.tierrahotels.com/atacama

7__India Tiger Safari

Following in the footsteps of Shah Jahan

A hundred years ago, there were tigers all over Rajasthan. Today, they are only to be found in the tiger reserves of Rajasthan's Ranthambore National Park. Spotting a tiger in the wild has become a rare privilege, and Aman-i-Khas Resort has built a special camp dedicated to this unique adventure. Historically, the rulers of Mughal Rajasthan, such as the legendary Shah Jahan, would camp in tents on extended tiger hunting expeditions, and the sumptuous tents of Aman-i-Khas have a clear sense of cultural continuity. Every guest gets their own tent, and each tent, believe it or not, has a verandah, a living area, a bathroom and a separate bedroom.

This is camping in the tradition of Shah Jahan. His tents featured various sumptuous rooms and glamourous chambers. "Roughing it" was definitely not part of the equation. When there were still plenty of tigers roaming the countryside, the Maharajas would live for months on end in their hunting tents. In other words, the experience of "glamping," which we think is so modern, was part of Rajasthan's culture long before the word was invented. Aman-i-Khas in India's Ranthambore forest recreates the mobile glamour and sophistication attached to a tiger hunt. The main difference today is that you shoot with a camera and not a gun.

___ www.aman.com/resorts/
aman-i-khas

8__Dhoni Sailing Safari

Island to island the traditional way

A *dhoni* is the traditional wooden fishing boat of the Maldives. Not too long ago, there were thousands of these double-ended, lateen-rigged vessels plying the waters of the Maldives. Before tourism, fishing was the mainstay of this island nation's economy. Tuna fishing, to be specific, was the main focus and work for the men, and the *dhoni* was well suited because it is sea-worthy and stable and still small enough to be handled by one or two people. The *dhoni* was everything: the mode of transport, the connection between islands, and the engine of the economy. Today, power boats have replaced the traditional boats, and tourism has now easily surpassed fishing as the main industry. But because *dhonis* are attractive to look at, even at anchor, most resorts have kept one or two, for mainly aesthetic reasons, and yet these traditional craft hold the key to an incredible adventure. The way that the Maldives has organized its tourism sector makes it incredibly well suited to a sailing safari. Each resort has its own island, and there is only one resort permitted by the government per island. So the idea is to visit a few different resorts by sailing to them. With the lateen-sail unfurled, it's not a big stretch to navigate from resort island to resort island. I cannot think of a more authentic or romantic way to explore the Maldives. You don't even have to steer the *dhoni* yourself. Just bring a local along to navigate. Create a list of resort islands you want to visit, book your next island in advance and go. This is the proper, Robinson Crusoe way to experience the Maldives, and yet almost no one is doing it. As an adventure, it is simplicity itself. All you need is a waterproof bag with a change of clothes, a toothbrush and a credit card.

—— www.comohotels.com/en/cocoaisland

LIKE A MOVIE

Exotic locations and breathtaking scenery are very much part of the modern movie experience. Who is Indiana Jones, after all, without the mysterious temples of lost civilizations? How exciting is James Bond if he just stayed at home in England? Many of the most spellbinding locations that play a big role in some of the world's most popular and engaging films, are real ... and you can make them part of your own adventure. Immerse yourself in the same exotic locations, create your own myth and star in your own epic tale. It's so much better than watching someone do it on screen.

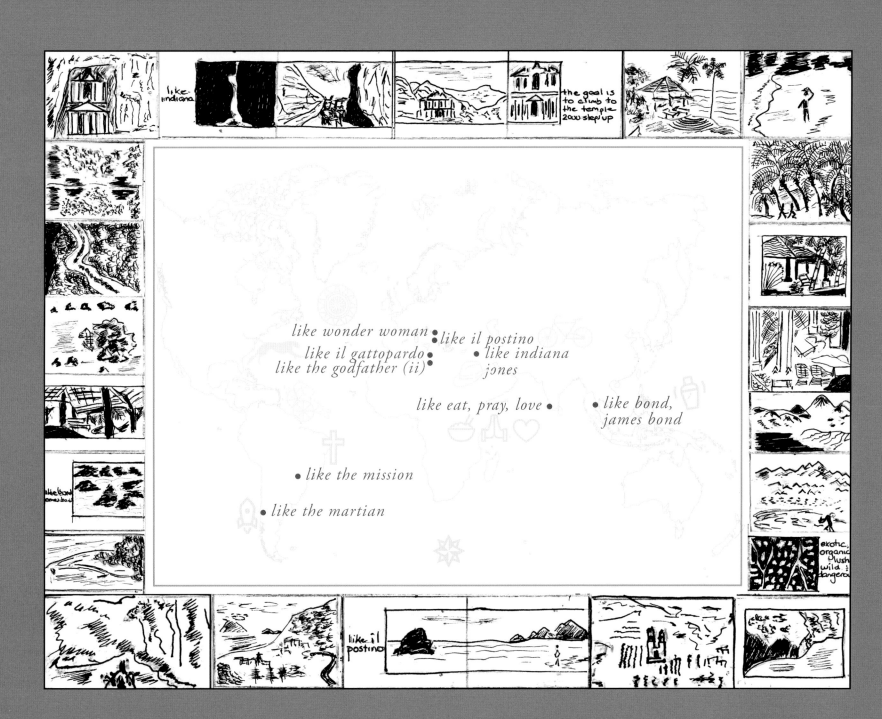

like wonder woman • like il postino
like il gattopardo • • like indiana
like the godfather (ii) • jones

like eat, pray, love • • like bond,
james bond

• like the mission

• like the martian

the goal is
to climb to
the temple
2000 steps up

like
indiana

like il
postino

exotic,
organic
lush
wild
dangero...

9__Like Indiana Jones

Starring in your own epic adventure

Indiana Jones and the Last Crusade would not have been much of a movie without the ancient city of Petra. It's as much the star as Indy himself. It adds the exotic to the equation and, in turn, generates the excitement. In real life, Petra is no less exotic or exciting, but there are some rules to follow to ensure it will be an unforgettable adventure for you. One, get there early. As early as possible. At the gates at 6:45am. Why so early? Because it gets hot, and it gets busy. There's a simple formula at play here. The more tourists around you, the less exotic and less special it becomes. At 7am, when Petra opens, it is empty – deserted. You can be the first to get to the Treasury, the famous structure that reveals itself through a narrow slit in a very tall, very dark canyon. Petra, like most imposing and ancient ruins, is spectacular, and silence and solitude help make it even more impressive. By the time more visitors start to reach the Treasury, you can be far away, having started the climb towards Ad Deir – 1,000 stone steps that snake their way through a seemingly impenetrable cluster of mountains that looks like it was made by stacking massive boulders awkwardly on top of one another. It's a spectacle and an adventure, that transports you back to biblical times, and yet there are none of the hallmarks usually associated with cultural treasures: no uniformed security, no plethora of rules and regulations, just one of the most magic places on the planet – as good as, or perhaps better, than anything you may have seen in the movie.

___ www.mainhotsprings.jo

Petra, as an experience, is pure theatre. This ancient city is only accessible via a series of very narrow gorges. These dark, mysterious tunnels of wavy striped stone eventually open out into ancient marvels of classical architecture, chiselled into the stone faces of the surrounding canyons.

10__Like Il Gattopardo

Living the life of a Sicilian aristocrat

Il Gattopardo (The Leopard) is Italy's best known book and most famous film directed by Luchino Visconti and starring Burt Lancaster and Alain Delon. The story chronicles the life of a Sicilian aristocratic family in the late 1800s, where their "day-to-day" consists only of lavish social events in spectacular palaces and regular sojourns to their imposing castles and farms in the countryside. The gap between the aristocracy that had grown very rich from their farms and the people working their land was more like a canyon. The book's author, Giuseppe Tomasi di Lampedusa, beautifully chronicles the dying days of Sicilian wealth and privilege, largely because he was an aristocrat himself. Castello di Falconara is straight out of the pages of *Il Gattopardo*: an imposing medieval castle, on the southern coast of Sicily, that belongs to Baron Chiaramonte Bordonaro. Built in the 14th century to protect against Barbary pirates, the castle was presented as a gift in 1392 to Ugone di Santapau from King Martin of Aragon as thanks for helping to protect the island from marauding invaders. The name given to this impressive, turreted stone pile stems from a later, more peaceful period when the castle was used for hunting – the square tower was where they trained falcons for the hunt. With its hunting trophies from the family's former coffee plantation in Kenya and its extensive collection of handmade, typically Neapolitan floor tiles, Castello di Falconara offers a rare insight into a world that has long since disappeared: the rich and aristocratic Sicily of yesteryear. Apparently, I was not the only photographer to appreciate its rare beauty. Shortly after my first visit, Mario Testino followed in my footsteps and booked Falconara for a fashion shoot for *Vogue*. Since my last visit, the castle has only got better. The baron has added a very beautiful swimming pool, nestled among the mature palms that define the garden, and I'm sure the secret internal passageway leading directly to the sea – a medieval gem – is now being used by guests to access the sandy beach just below the castle.

___ www.castellodifalconara.it

11__Like Eat Pray Love

Discovering yourself, in paradise

We have all dreamed of escaping to India, sitting under a palm, on a deserted beach, meditating, eating fresh fish and mangoes. Haven't we? It's the "hippy free love" escape. It's not about having a resort experience; it's not lying on a beach getting horribly sunburnt. I'm talking about taking the notion of spending the time to get in touch with yourself, to discover the spiritual you buried by a life obsessed with acquiring "things." In the dozens of times I have visited India, I have found some likely contenders to mimic the adventure like in the

book and film *Eat Pray Love*, but none seem to tick as many boxes as Surya Samudra. This gem is an old coconut plantation perched on a hill in Kerala that separates two sandy beaches – a big one and a small one. The guest houses are refashioned from traditional teak fisherman's huts, and there's a Ganesh-shaped swimming pool. Further up the hill, a small restaurant is fashioned from local stone. If you are really going to devote time to your soul and your spirituality, why not do it in style?

—— www.niraamaya.com/
surya-samudra-kovalam-resort

12__Like Il Postino

In the footsteps of Mario the Postman

Il Postino, the academy-award-winning Italian film, is the hopelessly romantic, thoroughly charming, and beautiful tale of Mario, the son of a simple fisherman, who delivers the mail on his bicycle on the Aeolian island of Salina. Via the letters he delivers, he becomes friends with exiled poet Pablo Neruda, who teaches him how to use language to seduce the woman of his dreams, Maria, the most beautiful girl on the island. Through Mario's mail rounds we, the audience, fall in love with the island as much as the story. Salina is beautiful in a way that is now rare in Europe. It is innocently simple – there are only two roads, a handful of vineyards and three villages on this volcanic dot in the Tyrrhenian Sea. Brightly-colored fishing boats rest on its rocky beaches, the sea is the very definition of Mediterranean Blue and tiny traditional houses cling to steep volcanic slopes covered in dense green. All I wanted was to do when I was there was to do what Mario did in the film: meander around the island on two wheels. I rented a bright red Vespa, put my camera bag between my legs, sat my wife on the back and together we followed in Mario's footsteps. We went to Pollara and swam in the crystal clear waters, we found the traditional granita vendor in town, rode up into the mountain's vineyards ... the only thing we didn't do was to give people their mail.

— www.hotelsignum.it

13__Like The Martian

The extreme sensation of a different planet

Being stranded alone on a distant, barren planet must be both scary and strangely compelling. Yet you don't really need to travel in space to find out. There is a place on Earth that so closely resembles the planet Mars (the Mars, that is, portrayed in *The Martian*, starring Matt Damon) that NASA has trained astronauts here in Chile's Atacama Desert to acclimatize them to the lack of worldly stimuli. More surprisingly, the comparison is not a recent thing. A hundred years ago, a Belgian priest, who was assigned to this, the driest place on the planet, was so convinced of the other worldliness of a nearby valley that he named it the Valley of Mars, or Valle de la Marte. But his Spanish wasn't great, or at least his accent wasn't, so the locals thought he was saying "Valle de La Muerte," or The Valley of Death, and the name has stuck ever since. Back then, either interpretation would have been hell, but today, you can wander around on Mars all you want, secure in the knowledge that there is a beautiful, cold, sparkling swimming pool waiting for you back at Tierra Atacama Hotel & Spa.

____ www.tierrahotels.com/atacama

14__Like The Godfather (II)

Experience the brutal beauty of Sicily

Sunburned, rustic and unspoilt, the Sicily where a young Michael Corleone is sent is a land of farms nestled into rugged mountains and quaint villages – an irresistibly romantic place. It is here, in this straw-coloured, sun-bleached landscape, that Corleone discovers the simple life: an agrarian existence dictated by the seasons. It's not surprising that he falls in love, and his wedding conjures up the epic charm of Sicily's forgotten farmland, with the men, dressed in slim, black suits and white shirts, shotguns casually slung over their shoulders, dancing with young Sophia Loren-lookalikes on stone-paved courtyards. Sicily's interior region has a timeless quality. Age-old villages perched on peaks stand guard over the fertile valleys below, connected by an ancient network of winding roads. The countryside is magnificent and empty, and it is not uncommon to be brought to a standstill by a shepherd crossing the road with his goats. It wasn't long ago that hundreds of people depended on Sicily's farms. Situated 1,000 metres above sea-level, not far from the town of Polizzi Generosa, Masseria Susafa is a massive farm – the kind of farm that made Sicily rich. One glance at the grain store, which is the size of a small cathedral, tells you this was once the backbone of Sicily's thriving agricultural economy. Owned for centuries by the Saeli-Rizzuto family, Masseria Susafa has been transformed by Manfredi Rizzuto Saeli into a guest experience today. There is something profound about staying here. You start to understand why many ancient civilizations tried so hard to take this land. It is not just fertile – it is vast and picturesque. The farmland here is more epic and more panoramic than almost anywhere else in Italy. The experience has been nicely rounded out by the conversion of the grain store into a restaurant and by the addition of a beautiful pool. As you drive through the remote mountainous landscape on your way to Masseria Susafa, the last things you would expect to find in *The Godfather* country are a gourmet experience and a turquoise pool with sweeping views.

— www.susafa.com

15__Like Bond, James Bond

Disappear into the exotic landscape of Phang Nga Bay

The 007 franchise has always thrilled, not just because of its "bad boy" British secret agent but also because of the breathtaking settings the movies consistently feature. One of the most memorable and exotic locations is Phang Nga Bay in Thailand, with its limestone karsts, or outcrops, which was chosen as a location for *The Man With The Golden Gun* (Kho Khao Phing Kan is now also known as "James Bond Island"). Karsts, the jagged monoliths with their patches of jungle cladding, standing like prehistoric sentinels in an emerald green sea, may look strange and foreboding, but they make for a wonderful playground. Every other limestone karst jutting vertically out of Phuket's Phang Nga Bay hides a beautifully deserted beach ideal for private picnics, overhanging limestone formations perfect for rock climbing and crystal clear lagoons ideal for snorkeling and diving. Because these giant structures also block wind and waves, the waters in between are also ideal for wakeboarding and waterskiing here in one of the most remarkable playgrounds in the world. I cannot think of a place better suited to your own Bond adventure.

www.sixsenses.com/en/resorts/yao-noi

16＿Like The Mission

Verdant beauty and monastic silence in the jungle

I don't remember much of the film's plot, but I do recall the priests (Robert De Niro and Jeremy Irons) dragging a heavy cross through thick jungle, past eerily quiet rivers and thunderously spectacular waterfalls in *The Mission*. The 1986 movie conjured a South America I wanted to visit, no matter the risk or danger. So I did. And thankfully, it was as much of an adventure as that of the priests – minus the humiliation and violence. It all starts with a short flight from Buenos Aires to Iguazu. Most of the passengers who disembark go straight to Iguazu Falls. I was the only one who didn't. Instead, I got the taxi to drop me at a clearing in the jungle, where I waited for a truck. This is the truck who takes you down a red-dirt road that goes on forever – two hours to be exact, but it feels like forever. By the time you arrive at a clearing alongside the Iguazu River, it is time to transfer your very red (from the dirt) self into a canoe. You're in

the back, and the guy who knows where he's going sits in the front. It's hot, very hot, the river is eerily silent, and the tiny canoe is scarily unstable, but no one can say this is not a real adventure. And there's a purpose to all this discomfort because this is the only way to get to Yacutinga Lodge. After an hour of paddling, you reach a small floating pontoon, or more accurately, the only pontoon for miles, and that is your arrival point. Someone from the lodge is there to greet you and take you straight to your bungalow. Then, you are invited to orientation drinks in a clearing in the jungle, which basically amounts to a log to sit on, a cold beer to drink and an extended lesson on local snakes. Perhaps unexpectedly, the jungle ultimately proved to be quite docile. I didn't see that many snakes, and we didn't lose anyone to a tropical disease. But it felt dangerous while I was there, which is definitely part of the appeal.

＿ www.yacutinga.com

Exotic, organic, lush, wild ... and dangerous, Yacutinga is the quintessential jungle lodge. You are in a jungle, in buildings made from the jungle. There is nothing here to suggest that there is a world of cities and cars somewhere. Here, it is just you, nature and wildlife. And that's the point. This is not just an escape from routine, it's a journey to a forgotten world.

17 __ Like Wonder Woman

Impressed by Ravello's Terrace of Infinity

The Terrace of Infinity is a panorama to beat all panoramas. It was Wagner's inspiration for *Ride of the Valkyries*, John Huston's setting for his 1953 adventure film *Beat The Devil*, and more recently the Hollywood stand-in for Wonder Woman's Amazonian Island in the 2017 movie. This extraordinary vista had a very ordinary start. Ernest William Beckett, 2nd Baron Grimthorpe, didn't do much right in his life. He was a notorious gambler and womanizer, he was kicked out of his family's bank for reckless spending, and he was forced to sell the family estate to cover his many debts. But in 1904, one thing he did that cannot be faulted was to buy a ruined farmhouse in Ravello, on Italy's Amalfi Coast, which he transformed in a magnificently exotic and eccentric manner. With the help of Nicola Mansi, a local barber-builder, he created a fantasy: a palace with towers and battlements expressed in an odd but somehow convincing mix of Moorish,

Venetian and Gothic architecture styles. And from a paddock where monks had once let their cows graze, he created a garden with Moorish tea houses and grottoes and classical statues and pavilions. The garden, which is now open to the public, is particularly renowned for its spectacular belvedere, the *Terrazzo dell'Infinito* (Terrace of Infinity). Lord Grimthorpe passed away in 1917, but his descendants managed to hang on to Villa Cimbrone, his creation, until the 1960s, when it was sold to the Vuilleumier family. They used it as a summer house and later transformed it into a luxurious hotel, which is what it is today. In the interim years, when Villa Cimbrone still belonged to Beckett's family, it played host to many famous names. Virginia Woolf, D. H. Lawrence, Henry Moore, T. S. Eliot, Jean Piaget, Winston Churchill and, most famously, Greta Garbo, who came here to escape from the press, were all much enamoured with Lord Grimthorpe's "folly".

___ www.hotelvillacimbrone.com

WILD SWIMMING

Swimming is an amazing way to discover places – especially places that are so well known that you might imagine there is nothing left to discover. Take London's Hyde Park for instance. Who knew that you could swim - wild swim - in Hyde Park? But you can, in a body of water known as the Serpentine. It looks like a lake, but it is actually a river; nonetheless it is a vast body of water in the heart of London, where you can swim to wherever you can row a boat. These swimming adventures have nothing to do with the boring repetition of swimming laps in a pool. Wild swimming is all about immersing yourself – literally – in locations worthy of adventure.

swimming with the swans
in london

swimming in brittany's
bay of the dead
swimming in the calanques
of the côte d'azur

swimming in lake como

swimming in the
grottos of capri

swimming under a
cathedral in mexico

swimming the walls
of dionysius

18__Swimming under a Cathedral in Mexico

Doing laps in Puebla's glass pool in the sky

This swimming adventure is sport, architecture, culture and travel all packed into the one very Mexican experience. The difference is the unlikely setting in a colonial water purification factory in the historic heart of Puebla, that has been transformed by the late, great Mexican architect Ricardo Legorreta - into an unusual and one-of-a-kind boutique hotel. Legorreta was a student of Luis Barragán, the Mexican architect who single-handedly invented a Mexican version of "modern." And so the massive courtyards, monumental stairs and striking use of colour that were very much the signature of Barragán – and later of Legorreta – are all part of the architectural package at La Purificadora Hotel. But the single best takeaway feature of this converted factory must surely be the glass-sided lap pool on the roof. From certain angles, the milky blue, transparent walls of this lap pool blend with the blue of the Puebla sky in a surreal fashion, and this long strip of blue water looks convincingly as if it is suspended beneath the ochre-coloured bell towers of the cathedral. You will never swim laps anywhere else in the world with such cultural overtones… swimming in the shadows of the cathedral, looking up towards the imposing bell towers as you turn your head from side to side … to breathe. It's a weird and strangely wonderful experience, especially since the transparent glass walls of the pool allow you to look at the people who are looking at you as you swim and as they drink at the hotel's adjacent rooftop bar. But even without the glass lap pool, Puebla has a lot to offer. The food, the vibrant colour of the town's historic architecture and the cool temperatures of the surrounding volcanic mountains make it a must on the list of places to visit in Mexico.

____ www.lapurificadora.com

19__ Swimming with the Swans in London

Submerging yourself in the Serpentine of Hyde Park

"Wild swimming" – in a body of water that's not a swimming pool – in London? Surely this is the very definition of an oxymoron. But not only is wild swimming in Central London a possibility, it is a surprisingly adventurous swimming experience. The location is a body of water called the Serpentine in London's famous Hyde Park. I had always assumed that the Serpentine was a lake, and the number of geese and swans that are in residence here made swimming one of the last things I thought of doing, until one day when I noticed some intrepid individuals diving into the water from a jetty on the south bank of the Serpentine. It was the first time I noticed the swimming jetty, and, upon closer inspection, I was surprised to find changing rooms, showers and even an official swimming club. "Dapper" and "eccentric" were the words that came to mind, but seeing someone swim in the Serpentine nonetheless piqued my curiosity. So I researched the concept, and to my surprise I

learned that the Serpentine is not a lake – it is a river. It's just that both ends – where the water flows in and where it flows out - are underground. The water, thus, is continually moving, so it is not dangerously stagnant, and, to my greater surprise, the water quality is rated by Thames Water as being just under drinking quality. So here it is, an amazing place to swim, hiding in plain sight in the very centre of London. Hyde Park's Serpentine not only offers wild swimming, but it also offers wild swimming without the boring drudgery of doing laps. From the swimming club's wooden jetty, you can head out to the stone suspension bridge that crosses the Serpentine and back. You're swimming in open water in the middle of the city, and it is deep enough that you never touch the bottom. In winter, you simply wear a wetsuit. You can add another layer to this adventure by cycling to the clubhouse. A wild open-air adventure in the middle of a world famous city. How cool is that?

__ www.serpentineswimmingclub.com

20__Swimming in Brittany's Bay of the Dead

A big beach with a scary name

Brittany is only five hours from Paris, but it is so different that it might as well be an eternity away. The coastline and wild landscapes that so bewitched artists such as Gauguin, Monet and Matisse are still just as they were then. This is the place where Gauguin's use of colour found its origins, and it could be said that the tone of 20th-century art was shaped, in part, by the natural beauty of Brittany itself. No wonder then that it is such a popular destination for adventure travel: a land of waves, unspoilt beaches and empty landscapes. There are many famous bays in Brittany, but none are as majestically beautiful as the Baie des Trépassés, or Bay of the Dead. Less than thirty minutes from the town of Douarnenez, the Baie des Trépassés is the most westerly point of Brittany, and it features a vast, sandy beach marooned between cliffs. It is an extraordinary location not just for surfing, but also for a dip in the sea. The name sounds ominous, but it is more due to a bad interpretation of the Breton language, a confusion between avon, which means "river," and anaon, meaning "the dead." The name "Bay of the Dead" almost certainly adds cachet for surfers, even though the waves are not that intimidating. After swimming or surfing, it's good to know that Ty Mad, one of Brittany's best and most charming boutique hotels, is nearby. "Ty Mad" means "good home" in Breton, and it is the perfect name for this small, stylish hotel tucked away on the picturesque coast of Douarnenez. The hotel has great food and a sandy beach of its own, and the house, a former rectory, is well suited to hosting guests because of its large size and great location. The personality of Ty Mad, with its original art, signature design and epicurean food, is a wonderful contrast to the epic, raw beauty of the Bay of the Dead. Combining swimming (and surfing) in the Bay of the Dead and lodging at Ty Mad - make for the perfect "action-gourmet" adventure.

__ www.hoteltymad.com

An epic beach with an epic name: Brittany's Bay of the Dead is so big that it takes ten minutes to walk from the carpark in the dunes to the edge of the water.
But the most epic part of this extraordinary beach is that you are likely to have it all to yourself.

21__Swimming in Lake Como

Immersed in Italian style and history

Lake Como was a favourite of Napoleon, Queen Victoria, and Tsar Nicholas, who were all drawn to its rare blend of majestic natural beauty and neoclassical splendour. William Wordsworth described Como as "a treasure whom the earth keeps to herself." So what is it that makes Lake Como such an enduring magnet for travellers past and present? The answer is the lake! There is something magical about it – it mesmerizes and captivates. You cannot tire of it because you never experience the same lake twice. It changes in colour and in texture with the skies, with the seasons and with the hours of the day. In winter, the lake is a symphony of solemn tones, and in summer, the bright light and clear skies make the water as blue as can be. Lake Como's natural beauty is captivating, but humans have also contributed to the enchantment. Baroque palaces with their elegant gardens, charming churches in picturesque villages and colourful houses painted red, yellow and ochre make this one of the most special places on the planet. Modest locals will tell you that there are some man-made structures around the lake that are not so pretty, but that's the point in a way: in the rest of the world people will comment on a building that is handsome or beautiful, but on Lake Como, they will talk about the few places that are not. Over the years, Lake Como has assembled its fair share of grand hotels. Villa d'Este, Villa Serbelloni and Grand Hotel Tremezzo all have a history of illustrious guests and memorable features that include swimming pools that float in the lake and elegantly manicured gardens. Opulent, chandelier-lit restaurants offer immaculate waiters clad in white dinner jackets, providing the kind of impeccable service that only Italians still seem to be able to sustain. Photos from the early 1900s are wonderfully revealing. Ladies in white linen and big hats on the tennis courts or taking tea on terraces overlooking the lake are a testament to how little has changed. In short, swimming in Lake Como is a timeless and enchanting adventure.

__ www.grandhoteltremezzo.com

22__Swimming in the Grottos of Capri

Splashing around in a cave of your own

The trick to extracting the most from Capri is to mimic the Italians who holiday here every summer. Do like they do: get a boat of your own. Hire one of the traditional boats that have been fishing these waters for centuries, a *gozzo caprese*. These small but seaworthy craft can get very close to the rocky shores of this "fabulous fleck in the Mediterranean" and are able to get in and out of Capri's numerous grottos without difficulty. Most of these *gozzi capresi* have been converted from fishing boats to pleasure craft simply by putting a daybed over the old fishhold. Normally, when you hire one of these boats for the day, it comes with a boat boy, a local who steers, operates the engine and knows the island like the back of his hand. Or, if you're the more adventurous type, you can hire a smaller version called the *lancia* and steer yourself (which is the cheaper option, starting at 70 euros, as opposed to 400 euros per day

for a *gozzo* with boat boy). A boat of your own is a day without agenda. The only decision you will have to make is whether you go around the island clockwise or anticlockwise. I would recommend clockwise because it's in sync with the sun. Once you are on the water, you decide what places you want to explore, stopping wherever you want for a swim in the clear waters surrounding the island. During this adventure, you are likely to pass the famous Grotta Azzurra (Blue Grotto), but I would avoid it because it is always clogged with tourists packed onto overcrowded boats. A better choice is the Grotta Verde (Green Grotto) on the other side of the island. One important thing to remember is to not ask your boat boy (if you have one) a question every few minutes. If you watch the Italians on vacation, you will notice that they do not speak to their boat boy unless it is to give directions, such as: "Stop, I want to swim here!"

__ www.capri.com/en/rent-boat-capri

23__Swimming the Walls of Dionysius

The ancient walls of an ancient city from the water

Dionysius I was the ruler of Syracuse, one of the most powerful city-states in the ancient Mediterranean world. Originally founded as a Corinthian colony by the Athenians, it prospered due to its unique location in the Mediterranean, situated at the "crossroads" of the ancient Mediterranean civilisations of the Phoenicians, the Carthaginians, the Egyptians, the Greeks, and the Romans. To protect this important city, the second largest in the Mediterranean at the time, Dionysius built a formidable 10-metre-high sea wall that still surrounds this ancient town today. It is this same wall that offers one of the most original swimming experiences in the Mediterranean. The adventure is to swim along the perimeter of this ancient structure, giving you a uniquely unusual perspective of one of the oldest cities in the world. Located at regular intervals, there are old wrought iron ladders that puncture the stone wall and allow you to climb down to the sea. These access points must rank as one of the more unusual ways to commence a swimming adventure. Once you are in the water, all you have to do is follow the wall. There is even a perfect little boutique hotel situated on this historic sea wall to use as your base. When I first visited Ortigia in 2001, Gutkowski was a boutique hotel on Lungomare di Levante Elio Vittorini, a street that runs along the top of the old sea wall, in a city that was in a state of semi-ruin at the time. Ortigia, the island on which old Syracuse was built, was halfway through a monumental restoration funded by a grant from the European Union. Fifteen years later, Hotel Gutkowski has expanded to thirty rooms, including the addition of its acclaimed GUT restaurant serving "neo-Sicilian" cuisine. The island itself is now full of interesting bars and great restaurants, as well as Sicilian baroque gems such as Syracuse Cathedral, which basks in the splendour of its newly completed restoration. This extraordinary church has some incredible features, including the surviving Doric columns of the original Temple of Athena, built in the 5th century B.C.

___ www.guthotel.it

24__Swimming in the Calanques of the Côte d'Azur

Diving into the fjords of France

A *calanque* is the Mediterranean version of a fjord. The most famous *calanques* on the Côte d'Azur are found between Marseille and Cassis, an area known as the Massif des Calanques. Like the Norwegian fjords, they are breathtakingly beautiful, and in order to protect them, France has established the area as a national park. There are also some *calanques*, still within the national park, beyond Cassis, just before the old shipbuilding town of La Ciotat. Calanque de Figuerolles in particular is popular with locals for cliff-jumping, freediving and spearfishing. A cascade of steep steps descends to a pebble beach and a narrow dark blue strip of the Mediterranean. Directly behind the beach is a small compound known as République Indépendante de Figuerolles (RIF), a cluster of charming garden bungalows clinging to the steep slopes of the *calanque*. It is a restaurant and a hotel that offers a refuge and a hideaway from the real world. RIF is everything you could hope to find on the Côte d'Azur. It's authentic, private and unspoilt. The food is fantastic, the rooms are "beach shack" chic, and best of all: you will have a *calanque* all to yourself! It is the perfect place for spearfishing. Equipped with big swim fins, camouflage wetsuits and shiny spearguns, you will slide quietly into the cool, deep waters of the Calanque de Figuerolles in pursuit of your silvery, slippery prey. It is said that fish caught by spearfishing taste better because they don't suffer the stress of being hooked in the mouth, which, apparently, causes the secretion of "undesirable" hormones. One thing is certain: catching fish by spearfishing is a lot more exotic than standing on a rock with a rod, waiting for something to happen. Spearfishing is not difficult to arrange, especially if you are a guest at RIF. You are allowed, by French law, to spearfish in the *calanques* from April until the end of October. Who knew that you could channel your inner mermaid or merman here on the Côte d'Azur?

___ www.figuerolles.com

SEEKING SPIRITUALITY

It is old … but it is also new. Some of the most exotic travel undertaken by humankind was in the name of spirituality. Adventure for faith dates back to the Crusades and well before. Seeking to understand the world through a search for meaning is as old as civilisation itself. Some would argue it is civilization itself.

In today's world, the quest to travel and understand people through experiencing their faith doesn't mean you have to "convert" to experience new meaning. In fact, the adventure of seeking spirituality asks nothing of you other than an open mind.

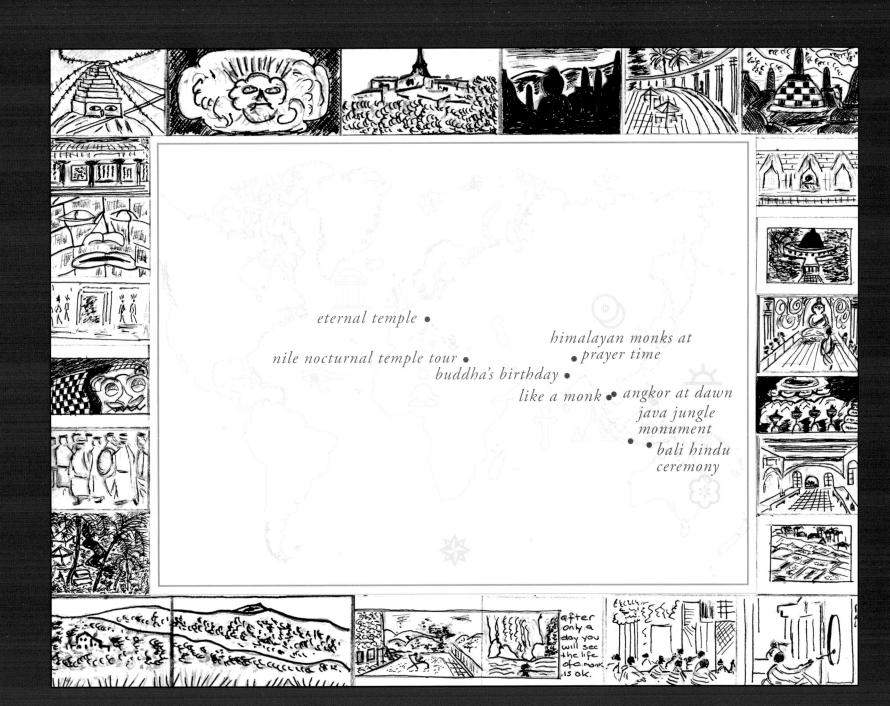

eternal temple •

himalayan monks at
• prayer time

nile nocturnal temple tour •

buddha's birthday •

like a monk •• angkor at dawn

java jungle
monument
•

• bali hindu
ceremony

after
only a
day you
will see
the life
of a monk
is ok.

25__Buddha's Birthday

Doing what Buddhists do on Buddha's special day

Buddha's birthday is a big deal, especially in Nepal. It's like Christmas without annoying jingles and greedy department stores. In Kathmandu, Buddha's birthday is a 24-hour street party. There is no organized prayer and certainly no solemn ritual. It's a party! So no one cares if you are a Buddhist… or not. For photographers – amateur or professional – it's a feast: a riot of color and pattern with flags and banners and strings of lights. It's an explosion of joy and exuberance. Taking part is simply a matter of wandering out into the streets. It really makes you wonder if this is how all religion really should be: a celebration, not a list of restrictions. The epicenter of all the festivities for Buddha's birthday is the Stupa, or prayer hall. You join in by walking around, clockwise, three times as a joyful meditation. It's just part of the fun, like a ribbon dance at a country fair. It's difficult to be specific about experiencing Buddha's birthday because most of it seems to be a case of "make it up as you go along." Is it an adventure? Absolutely! The adventure of doing something most of us hardly ever do – of just letting go and being spontaneous. There are no rules, apart from making as much noise as you can. There is, however, a formula for preparing for the day. Best to arrive a few days early and stay at Dwarika's, the most authentic and beautiful hotel in Kathmandu. Relax by the pool and eat in their restaurant, which specializes in local cuisine. Then you will be more acclimatized for the splendid chaos of Buddha's birthday. Arrange for the hotel to drive you to the Stupa, and that's all the planning you'll need.

____ www.dwarikas.com

26__Java Jungle Monument

Exploring in the footsteps of Sir Stamford Raffles

Deep in the mountainous jungle on the Indonesian island of Java lies the sacred and monumental Borobudur, the largest Buddhist temple in the world. It is a fascinating relic, made more impressive by the fact that it stands totally alone in the dense surrounding jungle. There are no other buildings: no houses, no reminders of any other time than the age wherein Buddhism conjured enough of a following to enable such a temple. By itself, Borobudur may not qualify as a true adventure because the entire site can be visited in just a few hours. What turns it into a proper adventure, then, is when it's combined with a stay at the nearby Amanjiwo Resort. A triumph of architecture, Amanjiwo not only reflects the shape and form of Borobudur, but it also functions as an observatory of sorts. From almost every space and location, Borobudur features in the distance. Amanjiwo almost feels like an extension of Borobudur. Despite its luxury and its beauty, it nonetheless radiates a profound sense of spirituality. You eat, you swim, and you relax in the exquisitely beautiful surroundings, but always in the presence of this extraordinary monument in the near distance. All in all, it's a spiritual journey, without a hint of sacrifice. Quite the opposite – it's difficult to imagine a place of more indulgent luxury, yet it all feels quite mystical, spiritual and exotic.

___ www.aman.com/resorts/amanjiwo

27__Like a (Franciscan) Monk

Silent dinners and days of solitude in remote Umbria

Silence, solitude and simplicity are what Eremito, tucked away in the wild hills of Umbria, is all about. *Eremito* means "hermit" in Italian, and that's the adventure on offer: the life of a hermit. This is a chance to reconnect with your inner spirituality, a brief period of redemption for your soul. It may sound a bit flaky or pretentious, but the reality is that it is fun and different, and you will definitely leave with feeling that you've experienced something unique and spiritual. Even if you only spend one night at Eremito, you will gain insight into the life of a monk. You sleep in a cell – a space just big enough for a single bed and a wash basin – and your meals are served at a large table under a tree. There are no options or choices, and their absence is strangely liberating. You eat what is put on the table, you drink the water from the terracotta jugs placed in front of you; the meat is organic and the fruit and vegetables they serve are seasonal. The staff serve the food and wine. Monks are there as guests (but not

always – it depends on occupancy…it is a boutique hotel after all.) To start a day without making decisions is wonderful. Afterwards, there are mountains and forest and a waterfall nearby, and you are encouraged to make use of them. I did all three by walking down the mountain and through the forest to swim in the ice-cold waterfall. At night, every night, dinner is a silent affair. You sit in a single row, side by side, and no one speaks … not a word … not you, nor the other guests, nor the people putting the food on the table. The next opportunity for conversation in on the terrace after dinner, and it is remarkable what a bonding experience a half an hour of pure silence can be. It is not something many of us have experienced, and that's what makes it special and memorable. It's exotic to have silence … it's liberating to have simplicity. There's great freedom attached to lack of choice, and yet the most revealing and indeed surprising insight from this adventure is how much fun it can be to live like a monk.

____ www.eremito.com

Every guest sleeps in a typical monk's cell. If you arrive with your partner, you get two cells. Every morning, breakfast is served at a big table under a tree with a sweeping view of the valley below. You don't get any options. You eat and drink what is put on the table. No choices or decisions to make – it is all as simple and uncomplicated as it can be. And that's what makes it so special and so soothing for the soul. An escape from the tyranny of choice.

28__Himalayan Monks at Prayer Time

The colour and cacophony of young Buddhist monks

When it was first suggested that I could visit a Himalayan monastery at prayer time, I thought of the experience purely in photographic terms. The crimson and saffron robes, the vivid patterns of the temple decoration, the gilding, the candles, the colors – all of this I could imagine. But never could I have imagined that it would be such fun. Normally, when we think of prayer time we think of quiet, sombre contemplation: serious and reverent to the point of fear. In a Buddhist temple in the Himalayas, prayer time is loud, raucous and very entertaining. The younger monks especially are rambunctious and mischievous, blowing as hard as they can on their brass horns, banging on a big gong, chanting loudly. Prayer time is a cacophony of noise in a hive of mischief. If only all religions had prayer time like this. What an outlet for youthful energy and exuberance. Visiting at prayer time is a captivating adventure, and you lose track of time as you are drawn into the chaos. It's an eye opener and a game changer. I don't agree with George Bernard Shaw in this case, as youth clearly is not wasted on these young monks.

____ www.pavilionshotels.com/himalayas

29__Angkor at Dawn

Ancient Khmer magnificence at sunrise

Angkor Wat, the ancient Khmer city in the jungle of Cambodia, is a vast complex that rivals the beauty and size of the Aztec ruins of Mexico and the Inca cities in Peru. It has become one of the most visited archaeological sites in Asia. Judging by the number of hotels that have popped up in Siem Reap over the last ten years, this trend is not about to abate, and for good reason. Angkor Wat is a place of extraordinary beauty and exquisite detail: a cacophony of *Apsaras*, dancing maidens delicately carved into seemingly endless stone corridors, and giant stone Buddha heads pieced together like enormous jigsaw puzzles that dominate bridges and buildings for miles. That said, the experience of Angkor can easily be diluted by the crowds. Ideally, it's a spiritual place best viewed in solitude and silence. That's easier said than done, but it is possible… if you know how. You need two things: someone who has a relationship with the monks who work as Angkor's caretakers and knowledge of the "trade entrance." The idea is to sneak in at 5am – before even the monks are awake – so that you are inside the ruins of this remarkable, ancient Khmer city when the first rays of horizontal light poke through the stone fretwork - an experience even most world leaders and billionaires have not had the privilege to experience.

___ www.aman.com/resorts/amansara

Surrounded by verdant jungle, Angkor Wat is one of the most impressive ruins in the world. This former city is a testament to the extraordinary civilisation of the Khmer. Although it is no longer inhabited, hundreds of monks are in residence to tend to the site. Most remarkable is the attention they lavish on broken and headless Buddhas. These statues were violently pushed from their plinths by invading armies that ultimately sacked the city, but the Monks dress the beheaded sculptures with the same care and respect that they bestow on intact sculptures.

30__Bali Hindu Ceremony

Witness a way of life on the Island of the Gods

The Balinese are deeply spiritual, and the epicenter of their spirituality is Ubud, the town in the jungle that sits under Mt Agung's mighty volcanic peak - the geographic center of the island. Even in today's electronic, social media culture, the Balinese version of the Hindu faith still plays an important role in the lives of villagers. There are ceremonies every week – you don't have to do much to experience one. And different villages have them on different days. No need to wait for the big Hindu holidays such as Nyepi. On Temple days, planned far in advance, villagers don their finest traditional clothes – the most elaborate and radiantly colorful silk dresses and fresh flowers for the women,

intricately tied headbands with Nehru-style silk jackets worn over ankle-length saris for the men – and take part in a showy parade to the temple, also decorated in flowers and silks. The procession includes drummers and dancers and bright parasols and flowers, and there's nothing rigid about it even though it is very well organized. These are processions of collective joy, expressed first and foremost as visual beauty. Unique in the world, these events are absolute feasts for photographers. There are not many places left on the planet where tradition and ritual still exist in all of their colorful glory, so a Temple day in Ubud certainly qualifies as a spiritual adventure not to be missed.

_____ www.comohotels.com/en/umaubud

31__Nile Nocturnal Temple Tour

The magic of Ancient Egypt after dark

Steaming down the Nile is a seductively timeless adventure. This river is the world's most ancient highway. The many temples that stand along its majestic banks have fascinated visitors as far back as the time of Ancient Rome and continue to do so until this day. But seeing these temples at night by the flickering light of a handheld torch is a different adventure altogether. You will not feel like a tourist. You will feel like a proper 19th-century explorer, minus the pith helmet. The steamship SS *Sudan* is the only vessel on the Nile that is allowed to visit the ancient temples after dark. The SS *Sudan*, built in the 1880s, is the steamship that was used to film Agatha Christie's *Death on the Nile* (1978), and it is still used today for excursions between Luxor and Aswan. En route, following a black tie dinner on the afterdeck, the steamship calls into important temples, such Kom Ombo, Edfu and Philae, to commence a small intimate visit. These nocturnal excursions comprise just the guests from dinner, a few flashlights and torches, and a whispering guide to orchestrate the experience. Why is he whispering? So as not to disturb the ghosts from the ancient past. Visiting the temples of Egypt at night is much more than a tour… it's an unforgettable and exotic adventure. Hieroglyphics, for instance, carved into the towering stone pillars of Edfu, are immediately a lot more mysterious when illuminated only by flashlight. The entire experience is a bit like a scary movie: thrilling and impossible to stop watching. To be honest, I didn't listen to a word the guide said, because I was too absorbed by the atmosphere. I was transported for a brief moment to the Egypt of Ramses and Cleopatra, to a civilisation that has left us pyramids, temples and sphinxes. To wander these places at night is to witness thousands of years of civilisation squeezed into a short but dramatic nocturnal adventure.

___ www.steam-ship-sudan.com

32__Eternal Temple

Ancient Rome's most impressive souvenir

Rome's Pantheon is an ancient masterpiece of engineering, built by Emperor Hadrian as a temple to pagan gods. It has stood unchanged in the same spot for two millennia. Most remarkable is the fact that the Pantheon's massive dome, which has a hole in the apex open to the sky, was made from moulded concrete lozenges. It remains the largest unreinforced concrete dome in the world. Who knew that concrete even existed in ancient Rome? Visitors through the centuries have been dumbfounded by the innovative construction and precise geometry of this extraordinary temple. And then there are those enormous granite columns: the soaring monoliths that would be difficult to quarry today, even with all the modern technology. To think how this was done in an age without cranes and hydraulics defies the imagination. The Pantheon is, without doubt, the most exceptional survivor from ancient Rome. If you visit nothing else in the Eternal City, you must experience this place. The Pantheon requires silence – an atmosphere of contemplation – if it is to be appreciated fully; it was a temple after all, and now, it is a church. Sadly, later in the day, especially in the warmer months, silence is simply not an option. The gravitas of this historic gem is drowned out by street vendors trying to sell you trinkets and flag-bearing guides yelling at their tourist troops. The best way to experience this ancient Roman masterpiece and to make it a real adventure is to get up by 7am and head for Piazza della Rotonda, home to the Pantheon. Grab a table at Scusate Il Ritardo (meaning "sorry to keep you waiting"), right next to the Pantheon, and order your cappuccino and a Nutella-filled *cornetto* (croissant). Now you can take your time to bask in the quiet beauty of this ancient place of worship and absorb the extraordinary sense of history. There is no better way to experience this ancient marvel than "Breakfast at the Pantheon."

—— www.hotellocarno.com

X CENTRIC

Exotic places should stimulate you to do exotic, eccentric things. It doesn't have to be something dangerous… just something different and original… and authentic. Sitting on a beach is not an adventure. It is certainly not something that will remain with you as a precious memory. Instead, you should be jumping off big boulders into the sea in Vietnam, or waterskiing in Turkey, or rock climbing in Oman or playing golf on an old tea plantation in China. The world is such a fascinating place, and there are so many things to do. It's all about experiences… not things.

- sunbathing in the palais-royal
- body boarding in • • fly-fishing in the auvergne
  soulac-sur-mer • riding white horses & tea plantation
  turkey water skiing • chasing black bulls • golf
  musandam rock climbing • • surfing goa's north coast
  vietnam rock jumping • yoga on the rocks

- andes hot springs soaking

- skiing in the high andes

33__Andes Hot Springs Soaking

In thermal waters on the roof of the world

This is hands down, without doubt, the most dramatic, the most inspiring and the most exotic natural hot springs experience you will have… in the entire world. It's a proper adventure that starts long before sunrise, at about four in the morning. That's when they bundle you into a car to start the 90-minute drive from San Pedro de Atacama straight up to El Tatio on the very roof of the Andes. Still in Chile. Just much higher. And you're a stone's throw from the border with Bolivia. When you arrive, just before sunrise on a plateau scattered with Inca ruins, at the unlikely altitude of 5,000 meters – the same altitude as Everest Base Camp – the temperature is hovering around 20 degrees below 0 (Celsius). This extreme cold magnifies the size of the plumes of steam that regularly explode out of the black volcanic ground. As the rising sun starts to cut in with almost purely horizontal bolts of light, the spectacle goes from impressive to mesmerizing. The El Tatio geysers are officially the third largest hot spring geysers in the world. But given the setting and the temperature, they are by far the most theatrical and impressive. I have been to Yellowstone numerous times, and the geysers there, although officially the largest in the world, do not compare to the drama of El Tatio exploding on the very roof of South America. Despite the bone-chilling temperature and the noticeable lack of oxygen, you should still bring a swimsuit because right there in the midst of the explosions and dense mushroom clouds surging higher than a 10-story building is a small, natural hot pool that you can swim in, surrounded by what can only be described as the extravaganza of an extraordinary natural phenomenon.

— www.tierrahotels.com/atacama

34__Vietnam Rock Jumping

Jumping for joy from big boulders in the sea

Jumping off giant rocks into the sea below is an act of pure joy. There's no reason to do it other than for fun, and it's even more so if the location is exotic. The best place I have ever found to do just that, with the biggest and most imposing rocks and the deepest (safe) water, is in Vietnam, on an isolated peninsula just north of the increasingly popular and touristy Nah Trang. The place is called Ninh Van Bay - a spot of exceptional rugged beauty with hand-built, wooden bungalows, based on traditional design, built into, around and on top of big granite boulders that define this stretch of coast. The boulders are stunning and monumental and sculptural, each shape offering a different experience in launching yourself into the sky below, like combining modern sculpture with exotic sport. Jumping from the boulders is not just fun… it's also a way to explore this fascinatingly different coastline. But why, you might ask, would you travel all the way to Vietnam just to jump off a bunch of rocks? My answer is this: what is it worth to feel like a kid again?

www.sixsenses.com/en/resorts/ninh-van-bay

35__Riding White Horses and Chasing Black Bulls

Cowboy for a day in the French Camargue

The Camargue is France's version of cowboy country. Camargue cowboys, known as *gardians*, spend their days chasing and rounding up black bulls – the ones used for bullfights. This unique part of France consists of more than 900 square kilometres of meadows, swamps, rivers and salt marshes. It is a natural habitat for herons, egrets, ducks and flamingos, and it is the only one of its kind in Europe. You can visit it on foot, on a bicycle or by boat, but the best way to explore the Camargue is on horseback. The Camargue horses are an ancient breed indigenous to the Rhône delta. For thousands of years, these hardy and agile *Equus caballus* have lived in these marshes and wetlands, developing their famed toughness and stamina. What is unique to this part of the world is that all Camargue horses are white. They are born with brown or black hair, which gradually turns white as they grow to adulthood. If you see a grey-coloured mount, for instance, it's a youngster. The adventure on offer here in the Camargue is

to be a gardian, or cowboy, for a day. It all starts at Manade Jacques Bon. A *manade*, in Provençal dialect, is a ranch. The mounts are ready early in the morning to avoid the midday heat, the saddles are Western, and the horses are trained to ride Western-style – reins in one hand to leave the other hand free. Once in the saddle, you quickly understand how much you will learn about this habitat because you're on horseback. For instance, who would imagine that black bulls like to hide? These strong, muscular beasts value their privacy, and they don't like to be disturbed, so they hide in the wild grass that is plentiful in this region – grass that is as high as a house. But if you ride into the grass, a somewhat intimidating experience, the bulls pop out, begrudgingly, from wherever they're hiding. "Cowboy for a day" means exploring, learning and doing something that is uniquely indigenous to the local culture of the Camargue. Doing it on horseback simply adds another dimension to the adventure.

___ www.masdepeint.com

36__Tea Plantation Golf

18 holes in a scene from a Chinese scroll painting

When do the words "culture" and "golf" ever appear in the same sentence? Never, except here at the Fuchun Resort in the ancient hills outside Hangzhou in Southern China. This is a golf course that oozes Chinese history and culture – like playing golf in an ancient Chinese scroll painting – as it snakes its way through an old, established tea plantation. The crisply-trimmed terraces define the boundary of the fairways, and the clubhouse and hotel were constructed in the style of a Taoist temple. The terrain is beautiful, authentic and imposingly memorable. And it makes you wonder why more golf clubs don't look at local communities and tradition and try to incorporate them into the creation of a golfing experience that adds more culture to the game. This unique project was funded by a Taiwanese billionaire, who prefers to invest in authentic Chinese history through real estate as a hobby. Arguably, Fuchun is his greatest success. He has managed to turn golf into an exotic, culturally evocative adventure… and, just as importantly, he has reintroduced the natural relationship the sport had with the landscape in the very beginning. Fuchun is true to the heritage of the game as well as the heritage of its location.

___ www.fuchunresort.com

37__Yoga on the Rocks

Striking a pose surrounded by the sea

You can do yoga anywhere. But I cannot think of a location for yoga that can compete with the gigantic boulders of Vietnam's Ninh Van Bay. This is yoga on top of Henry Moore-lookalike sculptures with a view of the turquoise waters of the South China Sea. Ninh Van Bay, about half an hour's drive from the seaside town of Nha Trang, is on a peninsula, but it is so isolated that it might as well be on an island. There are no roads to Ninh Van Bay – the only way to get there is by boat. And it is so well-camouflaged, set within and between the gigantic boulders that define this coast, that the entire resort is only noticeable once you get very close. The place is a testament to persistence and authenticity. Despite the challenges involved to get here, the guest bungalows were constructed in wood by traditional Vietnamese craftsmen using no nails, screws or glue. And they are spectacularly situated on top of, in between or under the boulders that resemble huge organic sculptures. Yoga on the rocks is not just a unique adventure. It's an extraordinary way to start a day in an extraordinary place. The boulders are all different in shape and size, and so it's entirely possible to do your yoga on a different rock every day. Ninh Van Bay has a spa and a dedicated yoga studio with instructors, but I do not think anything can compete with the boulders in the sea as a venue. Yoga is offered as an experience in many places around the world, but it is here, in Ninh Van Bay, that it turns into an adventure.

— www.sixsenses.com/en/resorts/ninh-van-bay

39__Musandam Rock Climbing

Ascending by climbing, descending by jumping

There's a raw, almost primordial attraction to climbing a rock. It is an intellectual as well as a physical challenge. Plus there's the danger that adds to the adrenaline rush – make a mistake, and you can hurt or, in an extreme case, kill yourself. That's the part I don't like. I appreciate and welcome the challenge… but I don't want to die for it. And that is what sets rock climbing on Oman's Musandam Peninsula apart. Make a mistake here, and you fall backwards into the deep seawater in the Gulf of Oman. And once you get to the top, jumping down is a lot more fun than climbing down. Like many, if not most of us, I don't really have a desire to make rock climbing "my sport", but I love the chance to try it in a real climbing scenario - not on a wall in some indoor gym with all the ropes and the gear. Out here in the ruggedly splendid landscape of Oman and wearing nothing more than some sneakers and some board shorts suits me just fine.

www.sixsenses.com/en/resorts/zighy-bay

40__Skiing in the High Andes

Relishing the spectacular peaks of South America

If you stumbled across one of the world's most beautiful and idyllic places to ski, how many people would you want to share it with? I imagine, if you're a keen skier and, like me, a keen avoider of crowds, the answer would be as few as possible. That's why Portillo, high in the Andes Mountains of Chile, is so special. It is not a resort. It is not even a town. Portillo is a hotel – a single, solitary, self-sufficient slab of a hotel – perched on the edge of beautiful Lake Inca at an altitude of 3,200 meters and surrounded by peaks that rise to 7,000 meters that host a network of different trails, slopes and pistes serviced by a surprisingly intricate web of lifts. All of it is owned by the hotel. That's what makes Portillo unique. If you want to ski here, you have to be a guest at the hotel. No exceptions. No day trippers from Santiago, and no skiers staying further down the road (there is no further down the road). And how many guests can the hotel accommodate? Four hundred! So, it follows that you will never share the mountain with more than four hundred other people. That's less than the average number of people standing in one lift queue in Europe. If you are one of the lucky four hundred, you won't exactly be roughing it. The hotel has two restaurants, three heated outdoor swimming pools on the edge of the lake, a full-sized indoor basketball court, a climbing wall, a state-of-the-art gym and a library. The food is amazing, and the service is legendary. My kids made a game out of the time it took for the food to arrive after ordering, and it usually averaged between 90 seconds and two minutes. Portillo is an extraordinary hotel in an extraordinary location playing host to some extraordinary skiing that is guaranteed not to be ruined by too many people. If that's not worth a flight to Santiago, I don't know what is.

— www.skiportillo.com

41__Surfing Goa's North Coast

Empty beaches and a colonial Portuguese fort

Goa is a different slice of India. Until 1961, it was not only a Portuguese colony, but also the Capital of the whole Portuguese empire in Asia. There are churches instead of temples, and many of the older residents still speak Portuguese. The architecture is an attractive mix of tropical Portuguese colonial with the distinct flair of India. With its swaying palms, white sandy beaches and exotic colonial heritage, it is no wonder that Goa became a popular counter-culture destination. Hippies were the first to discover its distinct charm, followed by the bohemian jet set and then by everyone else. Today, Goa is as popular with the people of India as it is with foreign bohemians. It is no longer unspoilt or undiscovered, but it can still conjure surprisingly exotic adventures. If you leave the hustle and bustle of Calangute Beach and head north towards the neighbouring state of Maharashtra, you will discover a part of Goa that has not been overtaken by tourism. You will know when you are almost there because a wide, fast flowing river will stop your northerly progress. The thing to do is to take the newly-completed bridge to the other side, then turn left and you will be heading straight for Fort Tiracol, an imposing colonial-Portuguese fort built on a headland by the river's mouth. This ruggedly handsome structure, built on the very point where the Indian Ocean meets the Terekhol River, offers sweeping and spectacular views of the pristine surrounding beaches that are – quite surprisingly – virtually empty. And even more surprising is the fact that no one is surfing the tidal sand break that leads to the river mouth. The surfing at Tiracol is average. But the setting is spectacular… and empty, which is what all surfers (including me) look for and dream about. Today, the fort is an exquisite boutique hotel. It is a small but monumental hideaway that is distinctly colonial on the outside and quite modern on the inside. It also happens to make the perfect base for a Goa surfing adventure.

___ www.forttiracol.in

42__Sunbathing in the Palais-Royal

Paris like you never imagined it could be

Paris is often sunny, and it can get quite hot in the summer. So where do you go to get some sun and cool down too in the middle of the city? The answer is The Palais-Royal, one of the best and least known spots to sunbathe in the city. It has fountains and trees and colonnades and tiny restaurants where you can eat outside and… it is as Parisian as it gets. Best of all: it costs nothing. Just grab a chair, park it next to the nearest fountain and your *séjour sous le soleil* is all set. The Palais-Royal is one of those places that could not be more Parisian. Saturated in history, dripping in glorious irony, this palace, originally built for a cardinal in the 17th century, was once a place for "sophisticated conversation" and "shameless debauchery." It was the destination of choice for aristocratic dandies during the day, and a favorite haunt for ladies of the night. Paris is so deeply ingrained in the Palais-Royal that you can feel the city's rich and extraordinary past radiate from the very walls. That's what makes something as simple as sunbathing here so special. You are in a place that has seen it all. In the late 18th century, most people visiting the Palais-Royal would have done anything to avoid the sun. The fact that it had a covered shopping arcade was a big part of its appeal. At a time when there were no pavements, and the streets were dirty and dangerous, the *galeries de bois*, as the covered arcade was then called, offered Parisians a warm, dry space, where they could wander freely to window-shop (a new concept) and socialize among the boutiques, cafés, bookshops and restaurants that quickly became the artistic and social centre of Paris life. The colonnades that define the Palais-Royal still remain, as do the many shops and eateries that continue to occupy the colonnaded spaces. Among them is the famous restaurant Le Grand Véfour, whose doors have been open in the same location at the Palais-Royal for more than 200 years.

www.hoteltherese.com

43__Body Boarding in Soulac-sur-Mer

Surfing in style on the silver coast

"Camping? I'm not camping!" That was the reaction of my teenage daughter when I announced that we were going camping in Soulac-sur-Mer. "This will be different," I said, trying to reassure her. "You will have your own bedroom, and there's a bathroom with a hot shower, and a big fully-equipped kitchen with a cosy corner for pre-surfing breakfast." "So we're not sleeping in a tent?" she asked, not entirely convinced. "No," I replied, "we have a bungalow with a view of the sea, a few hundred metres from the beach." I had taken my two teenagers on a "surfing and boogie-boarding safari"– a mission to find the best beaches and the best waves on France's Côte d'Argent, or the Silver Coast. Soulac-sur-Mer may not have the biggest waves, but it is certainly one of the prettiest spots, and the beach is huge and empty. At Soulac, it's all about the beach and the campsite called Les Sables d'Argent. The best bungalows are only a few metres from the beach, it is unspoilt and quiet, and in late June we had the place virtually to ourselves. It was warm and sunny, and our baby-blue bungalow was a stone's throw from the beach and the sea. My daughter had the biggest room, and my son and I shared a small room with twin beds. The bungalow was equipped with everything: coffee machine, fridge-freezer, microwave, gas stove, plates, glasses, pots and pans and a generous bathroom with a shower and plenty of hot water. Catering was easy. One trip to the Carrefour grocery store on the other side of town, and our dining needs were sorted. The only other decisions we were concerned with were the tide and the waves. The town of Soulac-sur-Mer is an old holiday destination with lots of beautifully preserved Belle Epoque wooden architecture. There are some charming restaurants, and there is a great *crêperie* in the centre of the old town. All you do is grab your board and make your way down the path to the broad, deserted beach. There, to one side of a half-submerged, concrete World War II bunker, you will find the ideal wave for bodyboarding.

___ www.sables-d-argent.com

44__Fly-fishing in the Auvergne

"Angling" for pleasure in the Patagonia of France

Patagonia is known as the Mecca for outdoor adventure and the place of pure nature because hardly anyone lives there – just like this part of the Auvergne in France. Hence the reference. Auvergne, in France's Massif Central, is a place of astonishing mountainous beauty with very few people and thousands of kilometres of fishable water. You could spend years fishing all over the region, and you would barely have scratched the surface. There are wild brown trout, grayling, Arctic char, carp, pike, zander and perch in abundance. As the locals say, "All the rivers have fish," and in the Cantal region alone, there are more than 60 streams that are home to legions of brown trout. There's something in the Auvergne to suit every angler, from the novice to the pro. As a guest of the eco lodge Instants d'Absolu, for instance, you need only walk out of the door with your rod, attach your chosen "fly" and cast your line. Or you can contact the Pays Gentiane tourist information centre at Riom-ès-Montagnes, which has a designated welcome area for anglers. You can drop in and pick up their hundred-page guide to the area's best fishing, and there's even a fly-tying station to help you make the most effective flies. At the tourist information centre, seek out a gentleman named Guillaume Vernet, who is very much the local expert. In a region that counts 50 freshwater lakes and two major rivers, as well as many streams, it's clear that there's no shortage of choice in the Auvergne, and since hardly anyone lives here, chances are you will have most of the fishing spots to yourself for your fly-fishing adventure. This part of France is also known for its medieval villages, built in sober grey stone, which have changed very little over the centuries. During the day, you can be immersed in majestic, unspoilt nature, and at night you get to experience a traditional France that is fast disappearing elsewhere.

—— www.ecolodge-france.com

ART ON VACATION

Art is as old as cave paintings. The desire to adorn and to express, through painting, sculpting, or other media, is universal. So it stands to reason that art can and should be an adventure. It is, after all, an important part of who we are as human beings. But museums have ruined it. They have turned art into a sanitised, rule-filled, "bureaucratic" experience that mainly involves trudging – with your arms folded politely behind your back – from one white-walled "boxy" space to the next. And yet, the world of artists such as Picasso, Gauguin and Van Gogh – to name but a few – was nothing like that. They lived for experience and beauty in landscape, in the culture of their surroundings, in food, in wine… in everything. Thankfully, there are many places in the world where art is still an adventure… and none are museums.

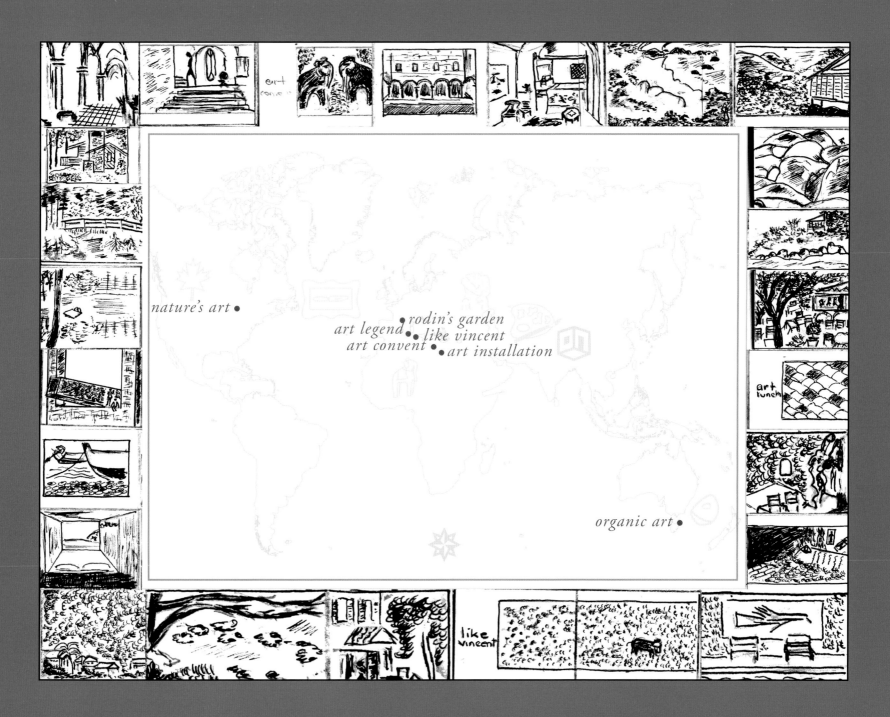

nature's art

rodin's garden
art legend
like vincent
art convent
art installation

organic art

art lunch

like vincent

45__Art Convent

An old Italian monastery and new African Naïve Art

In the very South of Puglia, at the bottom of Italy's heel and a stone's throw from the crystal blue Adriatic Sea, lies a 15th-century convent like you've never seen before. Il Convento di Santa Maria di Costantinopoli is a role model for how art can enhance life and a three-dimensional lesson in courage and daring when it comes to mixing history, art, interior design and restoration. When Lord Alistair and Lady Athena McAlpine found this convent, it was in ruin. Worse still, it was being used as a goat shed. Not ones to shy from a challenge, they set about restoring this thick-walled, Byzantine marvel. They kept the nuns' cells and the cloister and added a spectacular pool and modern plumbing. They did not install air conditioning, preferring to rely on the 2-to-3-foot-thick walls that have stood for almost six hundred years. But the thing that changed it from a pleasant historical place to stay into a genuine adventure is the art. Lord McAlpine was always a bit of a legend in the art world for his prescience. He collected Rothko long before the artist's work skyrocketed in value, and he would donate the collection to London's Tate Gallery. For Il Convento di Santa Maria di Costantinopoli, he and Lady Athena decided to use their unique collection of African naïve art, Aboriginal primitive art and soap advertising posters from India in the 1930s as the art that would give life to this imposing property. If you are even just vaguely interested in art, you cannot help but be mesmerised by the quantity, quality and diversity on display. It is staggering to imagine that two people collected all of these pieces in a relatively short period of time. Passion is a powerful motivator, and one thing is for sure: it rubs off on guests at this convent.

—— www.ilconventopuglia.com

46__Organic Art

More Henry Moore than Henry Moore

Sometimes, Mother Nature is both artist and muse. There is a place – an uninhabited slice of the north-east coast of Tasmania, three hundred miles from civilisation – where big boulders painted a deep red by nature sit on the edge of a blindingly white stretch of sand bordered by a cobalt sea. There is something overwhelmingly "artsy" about the aptly-named Bay of Fires. The shapes, the scale and the theatrical setting make these rocks more Henry Moore than Henry Moore. And the composition of the unlikely red boulders, the white sand, the green bush, the blue sea and a bluer than blue sky is testament to nature as the ultimate creator of still lives. You will wish you had brought your easel and paints. The rocks, for example, are a colour that Rothko himself would be jealous of, and yet they are simply the result of a particularly potent local algae. This place gives insight into how location can and has profoundly affected art, and it took the conviction of an artist to get the Bay of Fires Lodge – sticking out of the bush like a spear – built in the first place. It is the ultimate example of "touching the earth lightly." Nothing of the location was altered or damaged to build this lodge. There is no plumbing and no central electricity, and at the end of the season a helicopter removes the organic waste tanks. There's an extraordinary sensibility at play here, an inspirational example of the art of preserving and protecting some of Mother Nature's finest work.

____ www.taswalkingco.com.au/bay-of-fires-lodge-walk

47__Art for Lunch

Dining, surrounded by the very best of modern art

Love art, hate museums. I understand the educational aspect of "collections" and the role museums play in protecting, preserving and cataloguing our creative heritage, but they're boring. Walking around a building devoid of windows because daylight will degrade old paintings, devoid of furniture because they really don't want you to sit down and devoid of food because, God forbid, you might spill your soda on a priceless Picasso – it all seems counter to the spirit of art. Not so at La Colombe D'Or. This famous restaurant and hotel in Saint-Paul de Vence, in the hills above Nice in the South of France, has an art collection that rivals most museums. Matisse, Picasso, Léger, Calder, Delaunay – all the big names are here, and certainly not their second tier pieces. The giant mobile by the swimming pool, for instance, is one of Alexander Calder's best. The restaurant managed to accumulate all of this important art because the artists gave the work to the owner of the restaurant to pay their tabs. The descendants of the same family still own the property and still turn up every day to set the tables and serve lunch. I love their relationship with all this "priceless" art. They admire it, obviously, because it is the focus of the restaurant and the hotel, but they don't put it on a pedestal. They don't rope it off and pretend there is something holy about it. It's art, and it adds interest, enjoyment and culture to their restaurant… It's as simple as that.

___ www.la-colombe-dor.com

The typical terracotta roof tiles of La Colombe D'Or – in St Paul de Vence – are not typical at all. Yes, these are the type of roof tiles traditionally used in the region, but you will never find them in primary shades of red, blue, yellow and green. This roof tapestry reveals the signature of an artist, and this creative force was Monsieur Paul Roux, the man who opened this establishment. Now you know why Colombe D'Or was such a magnet for legendary artists such as Picasso, Matisse, Calder, and many others ... because the proprietor of their favourite restaurant was... one of them.

48__Nature's Art

The changing of the leaves, an annual spectacle

For a brief moment in time every autumn, the trees in North America put on a show. This is God's version of performance art – a spectacle of colour and hue. The intensity of the changing of the leaves varies by location but for some reason, the trees at Canoe Bay Hotel in Wisconsin seem to put on the most dramatic show of all. It may seem a stretch to call it an adventure to go "leaf peeping" here, but consider the location, which is something straight out of *On Golden Pond*, the reputation of the restaurant and the owner's passion for Frank Lloyd Wright architecture, and you start to grasp how the combination of all these ingredients makes it a genuine and unique experience. I'm a big believer in having the right platform to best be able to witness or observe an event, and Canoe Bay, without a doubt, is the best, most beautiful and most enjoyable venue for witnessing the changing of the leaves in the American Midwest.

——— www.canoebay.com

49__Like Vincent

When the South of France was famous for colour

Poor Vincent Van Gogh. What would he make of today's South of France? The yellow sunflower fields and purple lavender fields are still here, but the peace and quiet of rural village life is not. Today's South of France is a modern mélange of motorways, supermarkets, suburbs, hotels and tourists... lots of tourists. But there is one place that is entirely as it was in Vincent's time, almost 150 years ago. It's an island called Port Cros off the coast of Hyères. In 1960, the family that owned it gave it to the French State in a deed of gift. The deed specified that the French Government would need to commit resources, including an army of botanists and marine biologists, to return the island to its natural state. The state duly complied and continues to do so, and the number of visitors is strictly limited by one ferry per day. Passengers are counted when they embark and disembark, and no one is allowed to stay on the island overnight… unless you have booked a room at Le Manoir. Only this hunting lodge, still operated by the family that used to own the island, is allowed to accept paying guests, and therein lies the unique adventure of this place. Not only do you get a pristine island almost all to yourself, but you get to experience the South of France that inspired some of history's most important art.

__ www.hotel-lemanoirportcros.com

50__Art Installation

Interacting with art, not just looking at it

You know you are somewhere different when after breakfast they ask you, "Would you like to keep your plates, or smash them?" Excuse me? There's a giant kiln in the lobby of this hotel that "fires" the plates guests made. Plates that are then used to serve breakfast, or lunch and… you can keep them, you can break them. That's the way it works at the Atelier Sul Mare on the bay of Castel di Tusa, northwest of Palermo and 20 minutes from Cefalù. This is a place where art dictates every waking moment – not in a pretentious way but in a manner that children respond to, from a point of genuine curiosity and from the healthy perspective that art can be and should be… fun. And it is. There's a giant sculpture that kids can climb on at the beach, there's a kiln in the lobby, the bar was painted by young local graffiti artists and the guest rooms are not rooms… they are installations. There's a room covered top to toe in broken terracotta plates, a room that mimics a bird's nest, a room with walls covered in mud, a room that turns red when you turn the lights on. A cylinder-shaped room has a ceiling trap door for looking at the stars. Is it something you want to do at home? Certainly not. But that's not the point. The idea was to bring art into the lives of people who normally have nothing to do with it. Guests love it, especially the ones who normally have no connection to art. But there's something far more important at play here. It has changed people's perspective on art by making them part of it. Makes you wonder why it's not done more often.

— www.ateliersulmare.com

51__Rodin's Garden

Seduced by the beauty of sculpture in nature

Rodin, the famous sculptor best known for *The Thinker*, lived in a townhouse known as the Hôtel Biron on Rue de Varenne in Paris. This neoclassical *hôtel particulier*, or private mansion, with its elegant stone facade, built in 1727, was used as a Catholic convent until the school went bankrupt, and the sisters were evicted. In 1905, while a buyer was being sought, the property, along with its three rambling hectares of gardens, was leased to an ensemble of well-known artists. The residents at this time included Jean Cocteau, Henri Matisse and Auguste Rodin. In 1911, the Hôtel Biron was sold to the French government, and the artists in residence were asked to leave, which they did. All except Rodin. He had grown very fond of the place, especially the gardens that were so beautifully suited to his sculpture. So instead of leaving, he decided to negotiate with the government. What Rodin managed to achieve was his own immortality. The proposal he put to the government was simple. He agreed to bequeath all of his work to the French State in return for their commitment to cancel the sale of the Hôtel Biron, keep his work there and, upon his death, transform the property into a museum – the Rodin Museum. For the remainder of his life, he would also be granted the exclusive right to reside at the Hôtel Biron. His proposal was put to a vote in parliament, and the result was unanimous: the Hôtel Biron would become the Musée Rodin. François Auguste René Rodin passed away on 17 November 1917, and less than two years later, in 1919, the museum dedicated to one of the most important sculptors in history opened its doors. It is quite a story, and when you first wander through this immaculate sculpture garden on a sunny spring morning, you will understand why Rodin fought so hard for this place. In a city like Paris, full of sights that inspire and delight, it is hard to imagine a place that can compete with the magic of Rodin's sculpture garden. If you visit just one museum in Paris, make it this one!

___ www.musee-rodin.fr

GONE HIKING

Hiking in the wild is the original IMAX experience. It's a chance to immerse yourself in a real life panorama that slowly reveals itself as you engage in our oldest form of transport. Hiking is more than an adventure – it's a way of experiencing culture and landscape in a physically challenging and mentally rewarding manner. Hiking is a way to return to our primordial selves and give our minds and bodies a much-needed break from the sedentary, electronically-oriented world we live in.

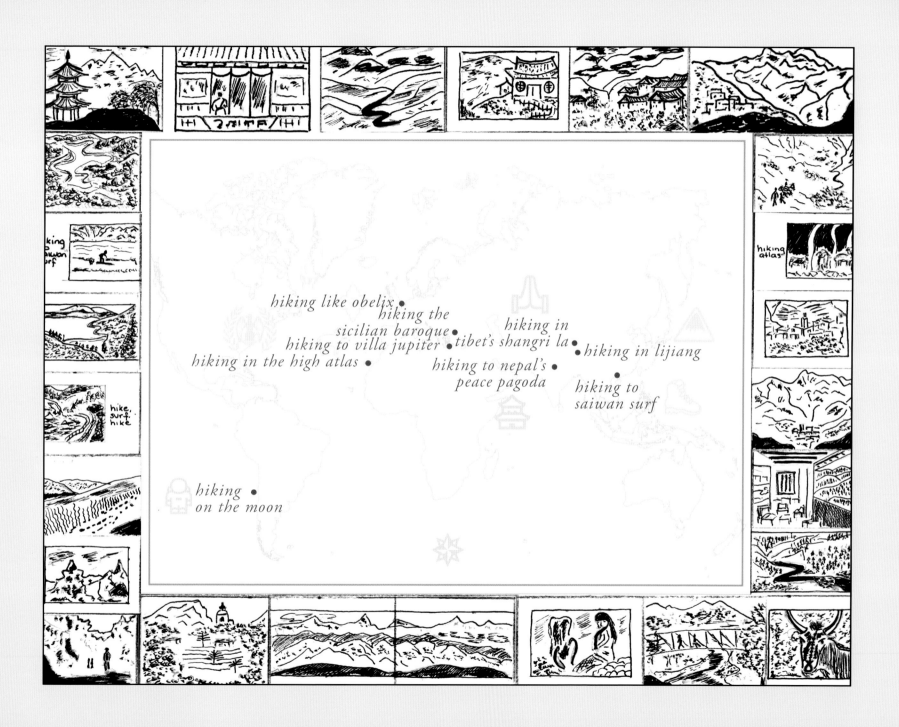

hiking like obelix

hiking the
sicilian baroque
hiking to villa jupiter

hiking in
tibet's shangri la

hiking in lijiang

hiking in the high atlas

hiking to nepal's
peace pagoda

hiking to
saiwan surf

hiking
on the moon

52__Hiking in Lijiang

China, at its most monumental

Judging by the expensive hiking boots worn by passengers on the flight from the nearest hub of Kun Ming, Lijiang is a popular destination for hikers - especially Chinese hikers. You may not have heard of it, but the Chinese love Lijiang. It's their Switzerland, famous for its natural alpine beauty. Because of the serendipitous fact that this part of China was the least affected by Chairman Mao's cultural revolution, much of the original architecture is still intact - so much so that most of the town is now protected by UNESCO. But most impressive is the natural beauty. Lijiang sits, famously, under the legendary Jade Dragon Snow Mountain, so named because its various peaks resemble the descending scales of a dragon's back. Hiking here is as varied and as challenging as you want to make it by your choice to hike through the surrounding foothills or embark on a serious trek into the mountains. Whatever you decide, you always have the history, charm and tradition of Lijiang to return to at night. It's an all-embracing experience that makes you feel as if you have stumbled onto the set of *Crouching Tiger, Hidden Dragon*.

—— www.banyantree.com/china/lijiang

53__Hiking the High Atlas

Trekking in the barren beauty of Morocco's mountains

Majestic snow-capped peaks, rugged landscapes, forgotten valleys, isolated villages, the high Atlas is hiking the way it should be: pure and unspoiled. Most visitors to Marrakech are surprised that these mountains are only a 90-minute drive from the city. The best hikes start in the tiny Berber town of Imlil, nestled into a narrow valley beneath the imposing peak of 4,800-metre Mt Toubkal. There are many directions, options, and itineraries on offer, but my absolute favorite is the climb to a refuge in a hidden, forgotten valley. The refuge is owned by Mike McHugo, an eccentric Driza Bone-clad enthusiast of the genuine and the authentic Morocco, who rescued the famous Kasbah Toubkal, the eagles' nest lodge residence of a former *caid* (chief), perched on a peak that overlooks the alpine Berber town of Imlil. So convincing is Kasbah Toubkal's exotic charm that film director Martin Scorsese chose this location to film *Kundun*, the

1997 film about the life of the Dalai Lama, because it looks more like Tibet than Tibet! From Imlil, my preferred hike takes you to a summit of 3,200 metres, a tough climb of three to four hours, where your Berber guides make a surprisingly sophisticated lunch, before departing for the three-hour descent to a tiny, mud village clinging to a mountainside and the home of your refuge. It's fascinating, challenging and... fun. The refuge is managed by a man named Mohammed, who makes a mean prune and lamb *tajine* and also prepares your hammam, the traditional Moroccan steam room. He also provides warm, woolen *djellabas* to wear at night. It was May when my kids, 13 and 12 at the time, and I took on this Lords of the Atlas adventure. When we woke the next morning, the ground was covered in a fresh layer of snow. Snow in Morocco? In May? Well, that's why this mountain range is known as the High Atlas.

___ www.kasbahtoubkal.com

The Atlas Mountains of Morocco don't get much attention or tourism. Few people know, for instance, that Mt Toubkal is almost as tall as the Mont Blanc in the Alps. Nor is it well known that it can snow here, even in May. The High Atlas is a ruggedly barren place punctuated by tiny mud-brick villages that blend into the mountains they cling to, and patches of verdant green created by bubbling creeks chiselling their way down from higher glaciers. For fans of dramatic and authentic hiking, there is no better destination.

151

54__Hiking to Nepal's Peace Pagoda

Ascending to the best view of Annapurna in Nepal

Not everyone goes to the Himalayas to climb Everest, K2 or Annapurna. There are other, less severe but nonetheless inspiring hikes to do, especially from the beautiful town of Pokhara. Here, in some of the most unspoiled countryside of Nepal, is a place that looks like a more exotic version of Switzerland. Your base is a charming cluster of beautiful bungalows called The First Pavilions of the Himalayas, tucked into a forgotten valley with green hills, great food, and a wonderful salt-water horizon pool. In the distance, high on a ridge framed by the snow-capped peak of Annapurna, the third highest peak in the Himalayas, is the distinctive white dome of the Peace Pagoda. The hike to this landmark is the perfect half-day adventure. If you leave early enough, you'll be back in time for lunch. You start, after leaving your compound, by crossing a suspended footbridge over a perfect silver stream, an immaculate little river that you should definitely swim in before you leave this idyllic valley. After the suspension bridge, the climb is tough and quite steep but not without unexpected entertainment, such as wild monkeys making a ruckus. Three hours later, you should have reached the Peace Pagoda. The reward for your perseverance and perspiration is a view of one the most impressive and sweeping panoramas of the Himalayas.

www.pavilionshotels.com/himalayas

55__Hiking like Obelix

Discovering the mystical magic of menhirs

I confess. I have read all *The Adventures of Asterix* books, and yet I know very little about menhirs. I know that the large stone that the character Obelix is always carrying is one, but that's about all I know. When I delved a bit deeper, I was relieved to discover that I'm not alone. A great mystery surrounds these ancient stones. We know how old they are (4500 B.C.), and we know that they were erected in huge numbers because so many survive to this day. But no one is entirely sure why they exist. The menhirs in the fields around Carnac, situated on the south coast of Brittany, are the most famous. Hewn from rock and planted in the ground, the Carnac stones were erected by the pre-Celtic people of Brittany and consist mainly of so-called "alignments," with the menhirs standing in lines like sentinels (as opposed to the circular formation of Stonehenge, UK). There have been some wonderful attempts to explain the menhir phenomenon at Carnac, but they are hardly scientific. There's the Christian myth that Pope Cornelius, upon being pursued by an army of pagan soldiers, turned them all to stone. Then, there's the Arthurian myth that Merlin turned a battalion of Roman soldiers into stone, hence the military precision of their arrangement. Scientifically speaking, there have been some attempts to solve the "menhir riddle." Many practical theories were explored, such as whether the stones had an astronomical role or a sacrificial purpose. No scientists, however, have been able to offer a conclusive explanation, but their efforts have helped to get the stones classified and protected. The alignment of menhirs at Carnac extends for more than four miles. There are more than 3,000 ancient stones here, arranged row after row with eerie precision. The mysterious nature of it all only adds to the thrill. That's what makes "hiking like Obelix" such an interesting and unusual adventure. Although it is only a short hike, it is well worth it. But be warned: go early, so you will be able to experience the supernatural atmosphere of this place without having to share it with too many others.

www.carnactourism.co.uk/discover/
menhirs-and-heritage/carnac-stones

56__Hiking the Sicilian Baroque

One hundred churches in one town

At one point in time – during the 1600s – Sicily was rich, the richest island in the Mediterranean. The money came from farms that grew wheat and from orchards that grew lemons. A lot of the wealth was spent on a beautifully and fantastically ornate building style that came to be known as the "Sicilian Baroque," a style that is unique to Sicily. Modica, with its abundance of more than one hundred fabulous churches and houses, is the best place to experience the Sicilian Baroque. The old town is like a monumental tableau of artfully carved stonework, squeezed into the steep face of a canyon and connected by countless flights of steps. It is a charismatic and unusual place to be hiking as a way of visiting the excess of its exquisitely-preserved historical architecture. Modica's compelling beauty is what inspired Viviana Haddad and Marco Giunta, two architects from Milan, to build Casa Talia as a place that would offer visitors the best experience of Modica. *Talia* means "look" or "admire" in the Sicilian dialect, which is the perfect name for this beautifully-designed compound. The 10 rooms, two houses and spectacular garden are all about the view: a spellbinding panorama of Sicilian Baroque at its best. The rooms of Casa Talia are set in meticulously-renovated cottages facing the old town. There are no churches or fancy townhouses on this side of the canyon, only workers' cottages built in a simple, rustic style. Working with an authentic menu of stone walls, lime plaster, cane ceilings and floors laid with traditional tiles, the architects have created an attractive and honest series of spaces that are reassuringly comfortable and also strikingly contemporary. The plates, the glasses, the cutlery, the furniture and even the food are as attractive, modern and original as they can be. Each room is unique, but they are all united by one thing: the captivating view of Modica's Sicilian Baroque. This is a hiking adventure of a different kind – a discovery of a forgotten history and style that is unique to Sicily.

___ www.casatalia.it

57__Hiking in Tibet's Shangri La

Black yaks and green mountain forests

Shangri La is the heavily-forested, greener slice of Tibet. This place is extraordinary not just because of its Alpine beauty, but also for the fact that trees here still manage to grow at an altitude of 4,000 metres - almost twice as high as the tree line in the rest of the world. Because of this altitude, however, you will definitely be hiking more slowly and for shorter distances, and it explains why there's a Thai spa in such a remote corner of the world to help you recover more quickly. Apart from the spa, this is a part of the world almost untouched by modernity. No electricity cables, no high-rise buildings, no motorways… just farms, yaks, rivers, streams and forests. This is a hiking destination of epic, unspoilt beauty. Yet the experience is not just defined by the surroundings. The accommodation also plays an important role. Looking out at the silver strand of a stream meandering its way through a slice of dense green pine forest, each guest at Banyan Tree Ringha gets an original Tibetan farmhouse to themselves. Rugged, colorful and devoid of internal walls - like a loft - these barn-like spaces are perfectly in tune with the surroundings. That's because they are authentic 300-year-old farmhouses that were painstakingly disassembled and then rebuilt in this idyllic location. The words that sum up the experience best are majestic and authentic: majestic views and surroundings, authentic food and lodgings.

__ www.banyantree.com/china/ringha

Shangri La – which means "paradise" in Sanskrit – is the most beautiful part of Tibet. Covered in dense forests of tall pines, it is a unique part of the world because trees normally don't grow at this altitude. Admittedly, hiking at almost 4,000 metres takes some getting used to, but Banyan Tree Ringha rewards your effort with what must be the world's highest spa. Spirituality, natural beauty, unspoilt landscapes and Yaks define what must surely be one of the most exotic and rewarding hiking experiences in the world.

58__Hiking to Saiwan Surf

Catching waves not far from Hong Kong Central

Hong Kong is not a place you associate with hiking, and yet almost every shopping center in this densely populated Asian metropolis has a hiking store. Why? Because it is surrounded by wild nature – by tall jungle-clad mountains, sandy beaches and countless picturesque coves. There are monkeys and wild boar and cobras, and the terrain varies from gentle to steep. Hong Kong offers a variety of different hikes, including a hike to a surf beach called Sai Wan. Who even knew that Hong Kong had surf? Sai Wan, in Hong Kong's Sai Kung East Country Park, is a remote crescent of pale sand and emerald waves surrounded by green mountains. You can get there on foot or by boat. There are no roads to this beach. The best way to go is by hiking because it is more interesting and more picturesque. An adventure before the adventure. No need to bring a board, as there's a place on the beach that rents longboards, boogie boards and stand up paddle boards. Although

it sounds exotic, which it is, this hike is remarkably easy to do. From Hong Kong, take the MTR (Hong Kong's state-of-the-art subway) from Central station to Hang Hau. Exit the station at Hang Hau, jump into a green taxi (not a red one - only green taxis know the way in the New Territories) and utter just two words to the driver: Sai Wan. He will drive you past the charming fishing village of Sai Kung and then deep into the National Park – it takes about 30 minutes total – which is closed to all traffic except taxis and minibuses. Then you'll reach a point where the road stops, and the trail to Sai Wan begins. The trail winds past a massive lake – Hong Kong's freshwater reservoir – through some beautifully lush forest and down to a beach that looks like it was transplanted from the southern coast of Australia. Ironically, even many residents of Hong Kong have no idea it exists. The people who do know about it would prefer to keep it Hong Kong's surfing secret.

www.thehousecollective.com/en/
the-upper-house
travelinsaikung.org.hk

59__Hiking on the Moon

Immersed in the monotone majesty of the Atacama

The name sounds like a Sting song, but it's not fantasy. There is a valley in the Atacama Desert of Chile called Valle de la Luna, or Valley of the Moon. It is monotone, like the moon – the rocks, the sand, the hills and the canyons are all the same color. And there are craters, like on the Moon. It's a strange but weirdly fascinating place to hike. The only discernible differences in such an otherwise colorless environment are the black streaks cast by shadows of yourself and other contours, and the faint white trails created by salt. In such a barren place, textures such as ripples in the sand become much more noticeable, as the deprivation sharpens your senses. But the real hook of this hiking adventure is not just the exotic monotone of the landscape, but the views that reveal themselves as you progress. Each time you hike out of a canyon and reach a new peak or a plateau, you stumble across a panorama of distant volcanic peaks dusted in snow and framed by cobalt blue sky, and red hills descending to glimmering salt flats… an extraordinary contrast with the landscape of the Valley of the Moon. Hence the illusion that you are on a distant planet looking out at other more colorful worlds. You will not likely get this impression from any other hike.

—— www.tierrahotels.com/atacama

60__Hiking to Capri's Villa Jupiter

Visiting the ruins of the palace of Emperor Tiberius

Hiking is not an activity anyone would associate with the island of Capri. That's what makes hiking to Villa Jupiter so special: hardly anyone knows about it. Villa Jupiter was the residence of Emperor Tiberius, and he ruled the Roman Empire from this palace, situated on the very peak of Capri, for 11 years (14 – 37 A.D.). Tiberius, successor of Augustus, was not a very popular or effective emperor. The great-uncle of Caligula and great-grand uncle of Nero was described as a dark and sombre ruler, but the one thing that made him stand out was that he abandoned Rome in favour of the isle of Capri. He ruled from the remote magnificence of the 7,000-square-metre Villa Jupiter on what is now Mount Tiberius, with a sweeping panoramic view of Naples, Mount Vesuvius, Ischia and the Bay of Salerno in the distance. You can visit the ruins of this infamous villa if you're up for the 45-minute, two-mile hike from Capri's Piazzetta. A series of narrow trails and fragrant pathways lead to the site, and on the way you will not only pass Villa Lysis, a neoclassical villa of the early 1900s made famous by the scandalized French author and aristocrat Count Jacques d'Adelswärd-Fersen. But even more interestingly, you will hike through the lesser-known Parco Astarita, which is still populated by wild goats – and it's safe to say that no one expects to come across wild goats on the isle of Capri. When you finally arrive at Villa Jupiter, it is impossible not to be impressed with the setting and the scale. From the reconstructed drawings that show the massive complex as it once would have been, it is clear that Tiberius was a man of taste. But to gain some insight into his character you need only seek out the vantage point known as Tiberius' Leap, with its 300-metre drop to the sea below. This is where disobedient servants and unpopular guests are said to have been given a simple choice: jump or be pushed!

www.capri.com/en/s/
villa-jovis-mount-tiberio

DESERT ISLAND

Books such as *Robinson Crusoe*… television series such as *Lost*… movies such as *Castaway*… they have all created a collective and enduring fascination with remote desert islands. These uninhabited patches of beach and jungle, usually in the tropics, surrounded by a turquoise sea, reflect not just our search for simplicity, purity and authenticity, but also our deep desire to escape. A desert island, it seems, is the perfect venue for an unforgettable adventure.

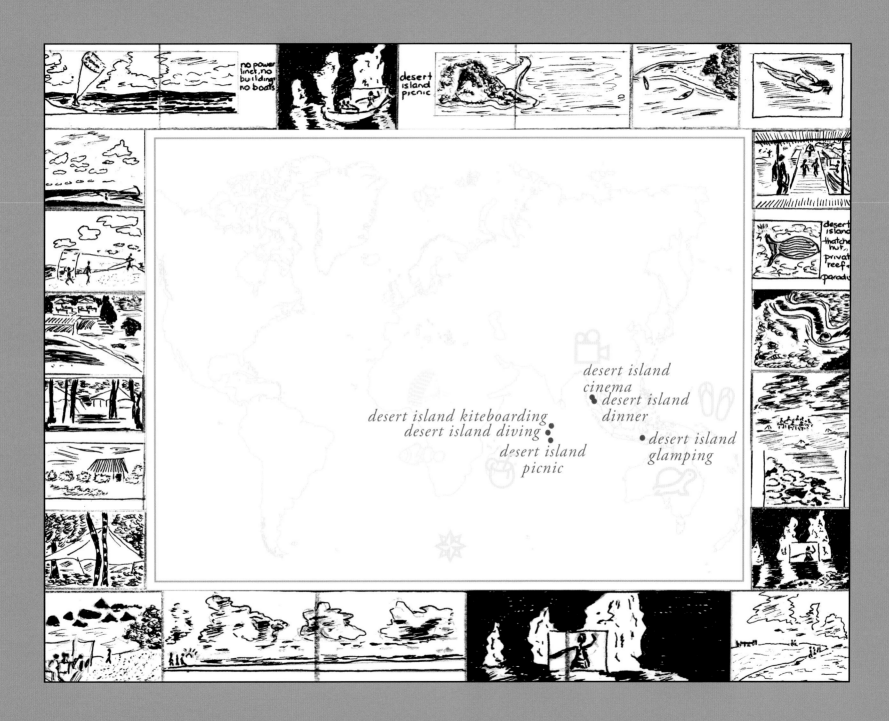

61__Kiteboarding without Obstacles

Learning without the danger of boats and buildings

A desert island is the perfect place to learn to kiteboard. You cannot be blown onto or into anything because there is nothing here… not nearby, not far away. And there is especially nothing to be scared or wary of – no power lines, no bridges, no apartment blocks. The water is warm and crystal clear, the bottom is sandy, and visibility is unencumbered in all directions. And unlike most kiteboarding destinations, here on the sand spit of Six Senses Laamu, you will not get entangled with or run over by other kiteboarders. A kiteboarding lesson on a patch of uninhabited powdery white sand in the Maldives consists of two steps: 1. learning to manoeuvre the kite on the sand, and 2. learning to manoeuvre the kite on the water while you're strapped to the board. If it sounds simple, that's because it is. You simply keep at it until you get it. The experience here is in sharp contrast with kiteboarding schools in Europe, where lessons are cumbersome, boring, safety obsessed and expensive, and you spend all your time learning what "not to do," so that by the time you finally get to try the sport, you are bored, exhausted, frustrated… and poor. Okay, kiteboarding isn't easy, but it helps if all the hazards are removed. On a desert island, it's just you, the board, the water and the wind. There are all sorts of travel souvenirs that are worthwhile. Having mastered kiteboarding must surely rank as one of the worthiest.

www.sixsenses.com/en/resorts/laamu

62—Red Lagoon Cinema

Watching a movie in exotic and epic surroundings

When was the last time watching a movie was an adventure for you? It's a rhetorical question, no need to reply. The inspiration behind this adventure was to create a "movie night" you will never forget. The idea is simple enough: take a desert island with a picturesque lagoon in the tropics, build a cinema screen in the water and use red-coloured spotlights to highlight the stunning limestone sentinels standing like sculptures in the black of night. This experience is installation art meets jungle cinema on a small, uninhabited island, with a sandy beach and some dramatic limestone outcrops in front of the beach in Pang Nga Bay, not far from Koh Ya Noi. Park the guests on mattresses on the beach, provide plenty of ice-cold champagne and delicious "finger food" – and voila! The logistics, however, proved slightly more challenging and complicated. A desert island has no power (logically), so a large (very large) industrial generator had to be brought in. But it had to be parked far enough away that you would hear nothing, which, for all intents and purposes, meant the other end of the island. Miles of electrical cable had to be laid through the jungle to reach the designated cinema beach. Then, divers had to lay giant scaffolding underwater because distance quickly minimises scale. If it seems extreme to put this much time, money and organisation into a movie night, don't forget this simple (clichéd?) aphorism, "The more you put in, the more you get out." Desert Island Cinema is an extraordinary effort and a remarkable act of untethered imagination that tested the resources and ingenuity of many. But it ranks as an adventure that is nothing short of monumental.

www.sixsenses.com/en/resorts/yao-noi

63__Castaway Dinner Club

Just you and your friends, alone in the world

Pure magic. Hands down, without a doubt, the most memorable dinner you have ever had. The formula is straightforward. Take an uninhabited spit of powdery white sand near Six Senses Laamu, surrounded by the turquoise waters of the Maldives' southern atolls. Transport yourself and your friends to "your sandbank" just before sunset and explore your private patch of paradise with a freshly mixed cocktail in your hand, provided by the staff who arrived hours earlier to prep for your dinner. Then, as darkness descends, and just as the sky starts to put on a spectacle that only the tropics can provide, sit down for dinner at an immaculately set table parked by the edge of lapping waves and surrounded by the romantic flicker of lanterns strategically buried in the sand. The chef and his assistants are installed just behind a small dune, out of sight, but just close enough to ensure the food doesn't arrive cold and the wine doesn't go warm. They serve tuna, the fish of the Maldives, and the wine is Cloudy Bay from New Zealand. I would trade this dinner for any dinner in any three-Michelin-star restaurant anywhere in the world... anytime. Eating is one thing, creating an experience you will never forget is another.

—— www.sixsenses.com/en/resorts/laamu

64_Glamping in Paradise

The luxury of a tent in the jungle

Glamping, or "glamorous camping," has become trendy. Mixing sophistication with a rugged, purposely simple way to spend the nights has appeal, but it does depend on your definition of glamour. I cannot imagine anyone not seeing this experience at Amanwana on Indonesia's Moyo Island as anything but glamping. Your tent is big and beautiful – and air conditioned. But that's just the beginning. The real glamour comes from the complete uniqueness of the experience. You are all but alone – with just a handful of other tents – on an island in the Indonesian Sea. Monkeys jump on your tent in the morning, sea turtles swim in the waters just off the beach and every other bird in the surrounding canopy of trees is an exotic or rare type of bird.

— www.aman.com/resorts/amanwana

65__Private Aquarium

Exploring a brave new world under the water

There are plenty of diving opportunities spread around the world, and this one is neither the deepest nor the most challenging. But it's probably one of the most enjoyable and certainly amongst the most unforgettable, primarily because it's so different from the usual diving boat experience. The small, fast, seaworthy powerboat is packed with more than just equipment. There are pillows, umbrellas and mattresses, as well as ice boxes packed with drinks and food. The boat takes off into the turquoise blue of the Maldives. Destination? An uninhabited sandbank in the middle of nowhere. This tiny island sports a bamboo shack and not much else. While the boat crew set up for lunch and prepare mattresses and pillows on the beach, the diving awaits on a private reef just offshore. A coral reef with a sea shelf that features eagle rays, manta rays, sharks and sea turtles that swim in the deeper, darker water, whilst the smaller, more colourful fish swim directly above and in between the brightly coloured coral. When you emerge from what is essentially your own private Nemo aquarium, lunch is being served in the bamboo shack. There's something very special about a private island and a private reef, as if you are the only ones left in the world. After lunch, we collected shells and picked up sculptural pieces of driftwood – more souvenirs, even though the day itself was plenty... for a lifetime.

www.sixsenses.com/en/resorts/laamu

66__Phang Nga Bay Picnic

A picnic as a postcard that you will never forget

Phuket's Phang Nga Bay must be one of the best places in the world for a desert island picnic. Each and every limestone outcrop – and there are many – hides an idyllic beach or a stunning lagoon, or both. So, there are countless opportunities for adventure here, and the strange thing is, very few people, if any, take advantage of it. Phang Nga Bay is not far from the mainstream life of Phuket, but most visitors, it would seem, stick to the island's increasingly touristy beaches. But the perfect desert island picnic is relatively easy to organise. You need a traditional Thai boat – and there are plenty of those – and you need some pillows, an awning or a couple of umbrellas, an ice box with drinks, an ice box with food, some flippers, a snorkel, dive mask and a swimsuit. Depending on where the boat picks you up, it will take 30 – 60 minutes to get to Phang Nga Bay. Once you are there, the only thing left to do is to decide which strip of pale sand flowing into the emerald water will be your private domain for the day. The boat will anchor on the beach, out of sight, and once you've set up, there's nothing left to do except explore, eat, snorkel… repeat! On the way home, you can ask your boat driver to take you for a tour of the bay. One thing I can guarantee is that this will be the most memorable picnic you have ever had.

www.sixsenses.com/en/resorts/
yao-noi

CULTURAL CONNECTION

Sometimes, getting there can be the adventure. Sadly, too often these days, transport is nothing more than a "necessary evil." Airport security is annoying, the flight is cramped, your seat is uncomfortable… but we put up with it because it's cheap. It gets us where we want to go. Luckily, there are still the odd examples left in the world of transport that are connected to the culture, and getting on that boat or train or truck turns the process of "getting there" into a rare instance of "being there." The transport itself becomes the adventure.

67__Nile Steamship Cruise

From Luxor to Aswan in vintage style

The SS *Sudan* is not the only boat to take tourists down the Nile, but it is definitely the only one that looks – and feels – right for such an ancient land. Somehow, river boats with DJs, trance music and AstroTurf on deck seem completely inappropriate. The best thing about this elegant steamship is that it is the most wonderful venue for doing nothing at all. Nothing except watching life on the Nile steam slowly by. Afternoon tea is served on the top deck at exactly the right time – about 4pm – and for once you need nothing to entertain you. A slow panorama of daily life constantly unfolds before you. Children swimming, farmers tending fields irrigated by the occasional flooding of the river, locals fishing and feluccas, the traditional sailing boats, carrying freight and people and animals from one side to the other. This river – the lifeblood of one of history's oldest and most famous civilizations – remains, thousands of years later, the focus of everyday life, and the source of everything vital and useful, from farming to fishing. As a passenger on the SS *Sudan*, you have the perfect platform and the perfect speed (slow and easy) to take in the ambience and the essence of the Nile. No wonder Agatha Christie was inspired enough to write *Death on the Nile* after she herself was a passenger in 1933. Scenes in the subsequent television adaptation and 2004 movie were filmed on board this vessel. I might add that in the story, the passengers hardly ever leave the ship – which I understand. It is cooler on the water, there's more to see and the SS *Sudan* is a beauty, especially inside. Where else do you get a panelled bedroom, a four-poster brass bed and a white marble bathroom?

___ www.steam-ship-sudan.com

The SS Sudan, an authentic Victorian steamship, embarks on Nile cruises between Luxor and Aswan. This is slow travel at its best, steaming quietly along on one of the most historic waterways in the world. The best part happens at night, as the SS Sudan is the only ship that has permission to pull up at famous archaeological sites at night. A tour by flashlight of temples built more than 4,000 years ago is something you will never forget.

68__Rickshaw Journey to Tiger Leaping Gorge

Mixing awe-inspiring nature with Chinese tradition

On a narrow path following the fast-flowing Yangtze River, they are quite a sight, lined up with their pink and red canopies waiting for their next customer. But there was no way I was going to take one. I preferred to walk to Tiger Leaping Gorge, the deepest gorge in the world. And I told them so with my best "hand" language. Unless you speak Mandarin, basic sign language is the only way to communicate. To which the Rickshaw drivers shrugged a nonchalant "suit yourself" gesture. "Why take a rickshaw when you can walk?" I asked myself. And now I know the answer to that question: because the famous gorge is very far away. As the narrow path winds around each bend created by the river, cutting through sheer faces of imposing mountains, you expect Tiger Leaping Gorge to reveal itself. But it doesn't. If I had known, particularly while lugging a bag of equipment, that the walk lasted more than an hour and a half, I would have gladly taken the rickshaw. At least I could have enjoyed the spectacular scenery along the way, which is the whole idea, I guess. Plus, there's the small matter of getting back. Unless you take a rickshaw to get there, you will not have a rickshaw to take you back. So I had another 90 minutes of walking back with a heavy camera bag to look forward to. How I envied all the people who were smart enough to say yes to the rickshaw. Because that is the experience as it should be. You can marvel at the sheer beauty of the surroundings, get blown away by the thunderous spectacle of Tiger Leaping Gorge and then enjoy, once again, the spectacular scenery in reverse, while being immersed in the novelty and authenticity of a real rickshaw. The point is this: of course a rickshaw is an outdated mode of transport, and of course it is no longer a regular transport fixture in China. But in this one, single, solitary, isolated instance, it is brilliant and appropriate and unforgettable.

www.banyantree.com/china/lijiang

69__Château Carriage Ride

Touring a French castle in a 19th-century carriage

Château de Canisy in Normandy is the real thing. It is still in the same family that has owned it for the past 400 years and although it accepts paying guests, it is definitely not a hotel. God forbid! Canisy is what it always was: a magnificent Château with all of its lakes, gardens and forests, intact. It is authentic in every sense; right down to the horse-drawn carriage that can take you for a post-breakfast tour of the property. This is something you should (must) do because it's an adventure back in time: you will see and experience a Château as it was meant to be experienced. From the first appearance of the turrets from behind the trees to the mist slowly lifting from the lake as the black swans start to glide across the sky reflected on the surface, you will witness the pomp and circumstance that made Château such as this the focal point and the "theatre" of 17th and 18th-century rural life in France.

The carriage is certainly not an "activity" invented to amuse the guests; nor is it a money-making venture. The upkeep of the horses alone renders it commercially unviable. Rather, it is something that is done because the family insists on hanging on to as much tradition as possible - no matter how impractical. The "horse and carriage" is part of the greater opportunity that Château Canisy represents: a chance to immerse yourself in the style and glamour of French history - a rare and remarkable survivor of an age that has passed. From breakfast served under massive chandeliers in the formal dining room to a delicately romantic dinner for two in the music room, to croquet on the lawn or fishing in the lake, to sleeping in sumptuous antique suites housed in imposing stone towers, Canisy offers one of the most romantic adventures there is to be had in France.

__ www.chateaudecanisy.com

70__ Venice Water Taxi

A gleaming mahogany boat for a city in a lagoon

In Venice, the water taxi *is* Venice. Everything that is different and exciting and memorable about Venice is embodied in these slick, gleaming mahogany vessels that power so elegantly through this one-of-a-kind "Rococo Water World." Where else on the planet can you step off a plane and straight onto a beautiful motorboat that can whisk you - via lagoon and canals - to the front door of your hotel or apartment? Yes, it's true: you could also opt for the vaporetto, the Venetian version of a bus. It's a public transport option that also travels on the water, but that's missing the point. Venice water taxis are not just about being on the water. They are about style and grace and extravagance. When was the last time you heard those words used to describe a taxi? Venetian taxi drivers are obsessed with their streamlined speedboats. They wash them, they polish them, they varnish them, they pamper them; they take pride in keeping them in immaculate condition. Why? Because they are Venetian, and Venetians throughout history have been obsessed with the water around them and with fine craftsmanship. A Venetian water taxi turns an airport commute into a thirty-minute adventure – a journey on waterways that have remained unchanged for hundreds of years. It's a cultural experience that substitutes for the usual and more mundane exercise of simply getting from Point A to Point B. In almost all other travel scenarios, the trip from the airport is something you'll probably want to forget. In Venice, it sets the tone. At least, it should. The price is fixed (around 120 Euros for the entire boat), so if you are with friends, the cost per person goes down accordingly. But even if you are on your own, it is worth it for the simple reason that it is unique. Splurging a bit on an experience you will never forget seems like money well spent.

___ www.venicewatertaxi.it

71__Naples Night Boat

Leaving Napoli at night to see Stromboli at dawn

One of the most appealing attractions of the Aeolian Islands is that they are difficult to reach. They are too small to host a landing strip and far enough away that even a "fast ferry" from Naples takes more than four hours. Because of this remote status, the night boat is a much more elegant and infinitely more interesting option. It departs from the Naples maritime passenger terminal at 8pm. If you've booked a first class cabin, which I would certainly recommend, as it's not expensive, you can expect a big porthole with a view out to sea, powder-blue linen sheets, down pillows and your own bathroom. The best part is the on-board steward gently knocking on your door at 5am to announce that the boat will shortly be docking at Stromboli. If you quickly scramble onto the top deck (and you must), you will witness the sun slowly rising over the fuming volcanic peak of the island, casting long horizontal bands of light onto the black sand beaches of Stromboli, just as the local fishermen prepare to launch their brightly-painted boats into the eerily-still waters of the Ionian Sea.

___ www.siremar.it

The most magical moment of the night boat from Napoli is when the steward knocks gently on your cabin door at 5am, whispering just one word: "Stromboli." The ferry that departed Napoli the previous evening is just about to dock on the volcanic island of Stromboli. If you scurry on deck, you will witness a sunrise of orange horizontal bands of early morning light illuminating a black volcanic island that is still smoking.

72__Western Saddle Expedition

Riding from homestead to homestead in remote Texas

The ranch is called Cibolo Creek, a spread in the Big Bend of Texas that is bigger than some European nations. Not so long ago, this was Comanche country, and the adobe buildings erected in the late 1800s that still stand were conceived with the idea of protecting the early settlers from Native Americans. Today, these thick walls protect mainly against the heat, and paying guests occupy the old fort and eat dinner in what was once the chapel. Yet, despite this gentrification, Cibolo Creek remains a working ranch. It's a cattle ranch that hosts two homesteads on either end, built to accommodate the practical task of moving the herd to spread the grazing – which explains the adventure on offer.

If you're not afraid of getting a bit sore in the saddle, you can take your horse and the beautiful, hand-tooled Western saddle the ranch gives you to use, and the supplies they pack for you, to ride to the other homestead on the other end of the property. It's a day's ride in a landscape straight out of *The Magnificent Seven*. You follow landmarks and creek-beds sketched on a rudimentary homemade map. Assuming you've not been distracted and didn't get lost, you will arrive at the other fort before sunset. I have never been a big fan of riding (horses) with no real destination. So I love the idea of using horse and saddle to go somewhere – to give you a day of *Once Upon a Time in the West* to have for yourself!

___ www.cibolocreekranch.com

GALLOPING GOURMET

Food is an essential part of travel. What you eat and where you eat can easily become one of the most memorable adventures you will ever have. I'm not talking about fancy restaurants with big reputations. I mean food as an experience, directly connected to a certain place. It can be simple, like homemade hot cakes at a ranch in the Rocky Mountains or an unforgettable pasta dish in a little place no one has ever heard of in Sicily. Food is like music; it communicates directly with the heart. Perhaps it's the ultimate romantic adventure.

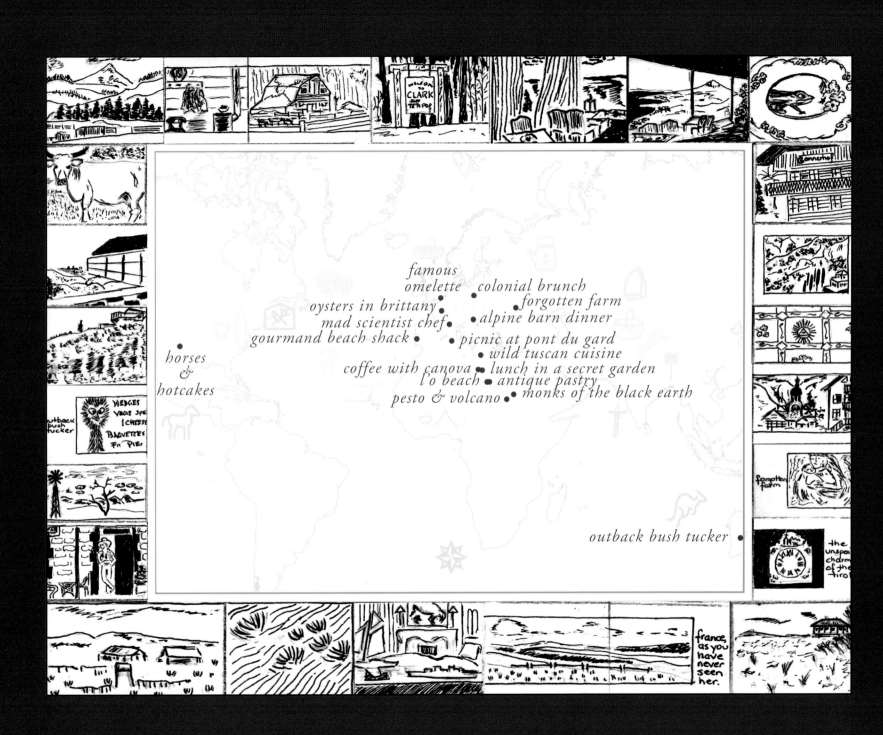

73__Horses & Hotcakes

Be a cowboy in the snow

Home Ranch, in the tiny town of Clark, just outside of Steamboat Springs in the Colorado Rockies, is not a fancy place. It's a ranch. There are horses to ride. In the winter, the foreman will throw your skis into the back of his pickup truck (everyone here has a pickup) and drive you to the nearest place to access the famous, powder-filled back bowls of Steamboat Springs for legendary skiing. "Back bowls" is a term familiar to skiers who like to go off-piste to ski untracked powder – which you will only find in the back bowls. The food, not surprisingly, is ranch-style: simple, homemade and delicious. It's how you expect a ranch, in the snow, in the American West, to be. And the best part of staying here is the breakfast. There's a big bell they clang in the morning whilst shouting out, "Hot cakes on the griddle... come and git it!" In the age of the ubiquitous "buffet breakfast," it's a nice change to sit down to eat something homemade that has just been "rustled up" in the kitchen – not to mention it's a hell of a lot tastier. And there is no lengthy monologue from the waiter because there are no waiters – just cooks and ranch hands. Years ago, it would have been strange to imagine pancakes straight from the griddle (with some bacon and eggs on the side) as a culinary adventure, but "real food" has become rare – and special.

____ www.homeranch.com

Framed by the snowy peaks of Colorado's Steamboat Springs, Home Ranch is the real thing. A place of weathered barns, horses, pick-up trucks and log cabins in the snow, this is how you imagine a ranch in the American West to be. The best part is when they clang the kitchen bell early in the morning, yelling the magic words, "Hotcakes on the grill, come and get it!"

74__The Most Famous Omelette in the World

More than a century of fame for one signature dish

Mont Saint-Michel ranks amongst the most visited monuments in France: a tiny medieval town squeezed onto a small island, topped by an imposing cathedral, surrounded by the sea at high tide and by vast expanses of sand at low water. It is also the home of one of the country's most enduringly famous restaurants. For more than a century, La Mère Poulard's legendary souf-fléd omelette has been sampled by kings, prime ministers, generals and presidents, as well as a host of actors, writers and other celebrities. And then, of course, there are the artists, who always seem to find the best and most consistent places to eat; Claude Monet, Pablo Picasso and Jean Cocteau all ate here. This renowned restaurant, situated within the medieval walls of Mont Saint-Michel, has been serving its signature dish since 1888. Annette Poulard, who was originally the personal cook of Édouard Corroyer, the architect who was entrusted with the restoration of the abbey of Mont Saint-Michel, started the humble inn. The spectac-ularly-located structure of Mont Saint-Michel had been allowed to fall into rack and ruin after the French Revolution, and at its lowest point, Mont Saint-Michel was being used as a jail. For Victor Hugo, author of *Les Misérables*, this state of affairs was too much. Horrified by the shabby treatment and subsequent deterioration of this unique landmark, he urged the French Government to do something about it. Corroyer was duly appointed, and while working on the restoration, he helped Annette Poulard to establish an inn within the walls of this famous religious destination. Her unique interpretation of a French classic – the omelette – earned her the honorary title of "Mère," as in the famous Mère Brazier of Lyon. To this day, the recipe of her creation, which is always cooked in a copper skillet over an open, wood-burning fire, has remained a closely guarded secret.

____ www.lamerepoulard.com

Mont Saint-Michel in Normandy is one of the most visited places in France – and for good reason. It hosts a cathedral on a hill, on a tiny island surrounded by a fortified medieval wall that has never been breached, surrounded by the sea at high tide, and by quicksand at low tide. There is nothing else like it in the world. It is impressive enough just to see it. But to eat a world-famous souffléd omelette at La Mère Poulard tucked inside this historic landmark, adds another level of adventure.

75__Pesto, Volcano & Coast

The best view of Etna and the best pesto in Sicily

I have travelled a lot in Italy… tens of thousands of miles in a rented Fiat Panda, dozens of train journeys and countless flights. I think I've been to every nook and cranny of this "old boot," and I've learned a few things. I know, for instance, that there is nowhere in Italy that can rival the view in Taormina – an eagle's nest perspective of a crinkly, turquoise blue, Sicilian coast framed by the smoking, smouldering, snowcapped peak of Etna, Europe's largest active volcano. It's a worthy setting for the best pasta I have ever had: the pasta pesto they serve at Villa Ducale, a small, elegant hotel in Taormina with a killer view of the famed volcano and coast. "Certo," you say. "Pasta pesto is an Italian classic!" Of course it is, but the pasta pesto at Villa Ducale is different. I could have it for breakfast. I loved it so much that I barged into the kitchen, compelled to tell the chef it was the most memorable pasta I'd ever had. When was the last time a dish made you do that? Why is this one so special? Because, instead of spaghetti, they use fusilli, and instead of crushed pine nuts they use pistachios, and instead of basil they use zucchini. Combined with the extraordinary view, it's a pasta pesto you are not likely to forget.

— www.villaducale.com

76___Forgotten Farm in a Hidden Valley

Authentic farm, authentic food, authentic location

It seems improbable that Austria, with its popularity as a winter ski destination, would still have the odd undiscovered valley. But it does. One in particular is called the Villgratental and even when you are actively looking for it, it's incredibly difficult to find. I know this because I once spent an entire day in the mountains driving past it. Or more accurately, driving past the well camouflaged entrance to the valley. Tucked into a forgotten corner of Austria's East Tyrol, the Villgratental hosts lumber yards and farms and a few tiny villages still dominated by their local church spire. In this authentic slice of forgotten Austria, you won't find apartment blocks or big ski hotels, but you will find Der Gannerhof, a restaurant in an old timber *bauernhaus* (farmhouse), which has earned a big reputation for the authenticity of its food. This is not a Michelin-starred establishment. It's a farmhouse with farmhouse food. Here, they make everything,

and I mean everything, themselves: the butter, the milk, the cheese, the bread and the jam. They grow all their own vegetables, pluck their own fruit from their own orchards and slaughter their own farm animals. When duck is on the menu at night, you know that the same duck (named Uschi) was still running around that morning at breakfast. Der Gannerhof is a proper adventure. It takes you to a place that none of us thought possible anymore: inside a self-sufficient farmhouse in an unspoilt, undeveloped corner of the Austrian Alps. Who amongst us even knows what food fresh from the farm tastes like anymore? It's a rhetorical question… we all know the answer. That's why this forgotten farm, hidden in a secret valley in Austria is such an unforgettable experience. Oh, and just so you know, there is skiing as well less than 20 minutes away. So, for once, you can have your cake and eat it too.

___ www.gannerhof.at

There are not many valleys in Austria that remain authentic and undiscovered. The Villgratental is so obscure that it's hard to find, even if you know where it is. This is Austria the way it used to be: a rural valley of lumberjacks and farmers, with hardly a trace of ski tourism to be found. This valley doesn't have much except a beautiful old church, some timber yards and an authentic old farmhouse called Der Gannerhof, which is not only one of the best places to eat in all of Austria, but it also happens to be one of the most charming and authentic places to stay.

77__Oysters in Brittany

Dining in a simple shucking shack

The Quiberon Peninsula is home to some of Brittany's most spectacular scenery. This is where you will find the intriguingly-named Côte Sauvage, or Savage Coast, and nearby are the legendary fields of Carnac, with rows and rows of monolithic, pre-Celtic stones called "menhirs" (think Asterix and Obelix). The Quiberon Peninsula also has a quieter side: the protected east coast, which hosts oyster fields in sweeping lagoons of azure blue. It's one of the most picturesque places to eat oysters in France. And the best place to eat oysters here is La Cabane à Jo, a shed where the oysters that grow on the surrounding oyster beds are sorted, cleaned and prepared. This shed, or *cabane*, is a simple, concrete box that happens to have magnificent views of the sea on the calm side of the Quiberon Peninsula. It is such an idyllic spot that it's easy to imagine it as the perfect place to eat oysters. And therein lies the simple genesis of La Cabane à Jo – a shack that is, hands down, the best place to eat oysters in Brittany. I'm not alone in thinking so. In 2018, La Cabane à Jo received a gold medal from the Salon International de l'Agriculture, or International Agricultural Show, in recognition of the quality of its oysters. Many of the world's top chefs will agree that "cooking is 80 per cent shopping." In other words, the ingredient is king! And in the case of La Cabane à Jo, the ingredient is the oyster. The word I would use to describe the experience is "pure." La Cabane à Jo provides the opportunity to eat oysters where they are grown, surrounded by a view that is perfection – nothing more than sea, sand and sky. It sounds singular, almost monastic, and that is actually part of the attraction. Yet, there is surprising sophistication to La Cabane's approach. You get to choose your preferred size of oyster, from 5 (the smallest) to 1 (the largest), and they are served with a pat of the most delicious Bretagne butter and a *baguette à l'ancienne*. The perfection is in the detail.

___ www.lacabaneajo.bzh

78__Mad Scientist Maestro

Indulging in the local cuisine of the Auvergne

The spaceship has landed… on a mountaintop deep in the remote rural province of Auvergne. This is a forgotten corner of France, where the ancient volcanic landscape has spawned famous mineral water brands, such as Vittel, and where there's a small village famous for its knife-making tradition – a brand called Laguiole. But the real attraction in this wild landscape is the unlikely presence of a steel and glass spear – an uncompromising piece of modernity – perched atop the mountain. It serves as the laboratory and showcase of a mad scientist, Chef Michel Bras, who has earned his three Michelin stars the hard way: without a hint of compromise. This is not a chef trying hard to impress with his version of the usual dishes. Instead, as a native of the Auvergne, he has dedicated himself to giving people a taste of

his "neck of the woods." It speaks volumes about his culinary talent and his approach that more than a decade and a half after being there, I can still remember each and every dish, like the starter called *gargouillou*, a salad of local, pastel-coloured wildflowers that looks more like a bouquet than an entrée. The mashed potato that is served after the main, like a cheese course, comes from a massive wooden bowl carried by two people. This dish is an unusual mix of potatoes and local cheese that you need to eat with a knife because the cheese is so blunt and rubbery. The *mousse au chocolat* is served with a "drinking cream" that tastes like liquorice because the local cows eat so much wild fennel. The experience is clever and interesting, and you learn so much about the Auvergne simply by eating here.

____ www.bras.fr/en/en-the-cuisine/en-michel-bras

79__L'O Beach

Sophisticated simplicity on a secret beach

Look for the Côte d'Azur on any map of France created before 1887, and you won't find it. That's because the name was an invention by the French author Stéphen Liégeard, who coined the term for his book titled *La Côte d'azur*. It is difficult to imagine a stretch of coast anywhere in the world that has had as much influence on modern culture. Authors such as F. Scott Fitzgerald wrote some of their most famous works here. And artists, including Picasso and Matisse, attracted by the climate and the colours, created some of their most famous work here. For many, the Cote D'Azur means yachts, film festivals and champagne, but there is also a Côte d'Azur that thrives on sophisticated simplicity, on experiences and adventures that have little to do with money and everything to do with authenticity – and romance. In an overlooked part of the Cote D'Azur, on a beach called Plage du Mourillon – a surprisingly pale and sandy crescent with almost no one on it – you will find L'O Beach, a restaurant that makes a detour to Toulon worth it. Created by a Toulon-based designer named Olivier Raymond, L'O Beach, in a sense, is the future of the Cote D'Azur: an attractive blend of modern design, Mediterranean produce and the exquisite flavours of Provence. It helps, of course, that the restaurant is… as the French say *pieds dans l'eau* (feet in the water) and that the beach, which is only an arm's length from the dining tables, is, by any standard, wonderfully and surprisingly uncrowded.

___ www.lo-beach-restaurant.eatbu.com

80__Outback Bush Tucker

Feral cuisine in Parachilna. Population: seven

Parachilna is a tiny town in what the Aussies refer to as "the back of beyond." The population, according to the sign, is seven. The only building of note is the typical Victorian pub made of stone, with the usual corrugated iron roof and a not-so-typical, award-winning, state-of-the-art guest house, an innovative structure half-buried in the ground to mitigate the intense heat. What, you may ask, is award-winning architecture doing here in the middle of nowhere, in a town of seven people? Who on earth would stay here? And why? The answer is simple: people come for the food. The Parachilna Pub, also known as the Prairie Hotel, is famous for its "feral cuisine." Wallaby burgers, camel sausages, emu egg omelettes, fried crocodile fillet, wild berry salads - all the dishes on offer can be found in the wild, right here in the Australian bush; hence, "feral." Add to this the experience of the Outback: the complete silence of a stark landscape, the surprising magnificence of a sandy world, and you start to understand the attraction of Parachilna and its "bush tucker." But don't take my word for it. Ask Kate Winslet, Harvey Keitel and a host of other famous actors and film directors who have stayed at the Prairie Hotel because, in addition to its culinary credentials, Parachilna has also made a name for itself as the preferred Outback location for movies such as *Rabbit-Proof Fence* and *Holy Smoke*.

__ www.prairiehotel.com.au

81__Lunch in a Secret Garden

The spectacular gardens of Hotel de Russie

You could visit Rome on numerous occasions and never know it's there. You could walk from Piazza del Popolo to the Spanish Steps and be completely unaware that an extraordinary garden exists just behind the imposing stone façades of Via del Babuino. The fall of the Roman Empire left the "Eternal City" in ruins, and Rome would have to wait another thousand years for the Catholic Church to pick up the beautification baton. Renaissance cardinals and popes commissioned handsome buildings, splendid monuments and, in some cases, spectacular gardens. The most prolific patron of all was Cardinal Scipione Borghese, who, in the early 17th century, spent vast sums on turning his former vineyard into the most extensive garden complex to be conceived in Rome since the days of antiquity. His legacy survives today as the Borghese Gardens, a splendid public park of more than 80 hectares, at the top of Rome's Pincian Hill. What

is not commonly known, though, is that a small part of Borghese's botanical creation still exists as a *giardino segreto*, or secret garden. Completely obscured from public view by the façade of grand Hotel de Russie, the garden is a remarkable backdrop for one of Rome's best restaurants, Le Jardin de Russie. This is a world within a world. While the rest of Rome might be noisy, busy and hot, this secret garden is cool and serene. It has terraces complete with fountains, stone steps and marble balustrades chiselled into the steep face of the Pincian Hill, enveloping the dinner guest in what amounts to a monumental theatre of green. Between April and November, I cannot think of a more beautiful or enchanting place in Rome to eat. Try the octopus and cuttlefish *alla cacciatora*, or pici pasta with shrimp and pistachios, and be sure to have the fig tart with a glass of Brachetto for dessert. If you have lunch only once in Rome, make sure it is here.

www.roccofortehotels.com/
hotels-and-resorts/hotel-de-russie

5☾

82__Ancient Roman Pastry

A recipe from 2,500 years ago

Ancient Rome and modern Rome live side by side in the "Eternal City." You can walk around remarkably intact remnants of the Roman Empire in what was the world's first metropolis, such as the monumental Colosseum, a stadium that would be impressive even by today's standards, or the Parthenon, a temple so perfectly preserved that it's hard to imagine that it has been standing for more than 2,000 years. Then go shopping in well-known Italian boutiques, such as Gucci, Dolce & Gabbana, Loro Piana, Fendi, and Brunello Cuccinelli, on fashionable Via Condotti. You can touch ancient Rome, you can walk around Ancient Rome, you can marvel at Ancient Rome – but who knew that you can also taste Ancient Rome? There is one tiny *pasticceria*, or bakery – not much bigger than a walk-in closet – near Piazza Navona that makes a pastry exactly the way it was made 2,000 years ago. Pasticceria 5 Lune bakes a pastry called *dolci antichi*, and it is made with filo pastry folded around a core of ricotta cheese, honey, black cherries, and sage. It looks like something you would find in Greece, which makes sense because Ancient Romans were very good at copying everything from Ancient Greece. This antique pastry is more than an interesting dish to eat; it's an intimate connection with ancient Rome. *Dolci antichi* is delicious, but what is fascinating is that it is also current and modern too. It is made with no added sugar, no preservatives and nothing artificial. You could serve it in a groovy, contemporary café somewhere in a big city, and no one would guess that this is a pastry made from an ancient Roman recipe. The best way to enjoy this sweet treat from antiquity is to combine it with a cappuccino, but 5 Lune doesn't have a coffee machine (it's a *pasticceria*, not a café), so buy your pastries, take them to the café just next door and order your cappuccino, and enjoy your small slice of 2,000-year-old Rome. *Dolci antichi* is a delicious reminder of just how civilised Ancient Rome really was.

___ www.5luneroma.it

83__Gourmand Beach Shack

A gourmet hunting lodge in the dunes of Les Landes

This is a France you have seldom seen: empty, pristine, with no cafés, no villages and no people… just wild dunes, clear beaches and the occasional hunting lodge. This area, on the west coast of France, just north of Biarritz, is called Les Landes, and the French Government got busy years ago turning this patch of sandy coastline into a national park and nature reserve. The only buildings that are still allowed inside the park are the wooden hunting lodges that were originally built in the 19th century. That's why this lodge, the Huchet Beach House, is so rare. Wooden anomalies like this are certainly few and far between, but rarer still is the food on offer. Huchet Beach House belongs to Michel Guérard, one of the original super chefs of France, who has had three Michelin stars longer than anyone can remember for his famous Cuisine Minceur at his restaurant and spa Eugénie-Les-Bains in the foothills of the Pyrenees. He acquired this old hunting lodge in the dunes of Les Landes to supplement the spa experience of his hotel and restaurant – a way to recover from a world where we eat and sleep badly. Except at this beach shack, you have food from one of the world's most celebrated chefs.

www.lespresdeugenie.com/en/beach-house/history-lodge

84__Monks of the Black Earth

Organic wine and cuisine under smoking Mt. Etna

With a name as theatrical as Monks of the Black Earth, you'd expect something special or unusual from this property at the very least. In the 18th century, Franciscan monks came here, to the rich volcanic slopes just under Mount Etna, to work the land. With sweat and toil, they built terraces of black lava stone overlooking the Mediterranean below, and they cultivated vineyards in the shadows of the smoking peak of Etna. When this order of Franciscan monks died out, the carefully-constructed terraces were left unattended for centuries – until the day that Guido Coffa found this abandoned, overgrown vineyard while exploring the area on his scooter. What he had stumbled across was a 24-hectare farm with a dilapidated, 19th-century house and a series of cottages in total disrepair. Despite the state of ruin, he purchased the property and put a plan in place to rebuild the terrace walls, replant vines, renovate the

main house and fix up the cottages. The list of things to do was long, but Guido did them all and more with the focus on the agriculture. Monaci delle Terre Nere, or Monks of the Black Earth, makes its own wine from grapes grown on its restored terraces, and it grows its own organic produce, served in its celebrated restaurant, Locanda Nerello. Monaci is an amazing place to stay that also happens to serve delicious organic food and wine. This is not your typical agritourism experience. You are the guest of a farmer, but this farmer is as serious about design as he is about agriculture. The converted lava stone cottages are authentic and rustic on the outside and as modern as it gets on the inside. This is the kind of place that gives you the ultimate Etna experience: sweeping views, historic vineyards, authentic architecture and a fuming volcano breathing down on your organic breakfast in the garden.

—— www.monacidelleterrenere.it

85__Wild Tuscan Cuisine

Foraging for culinary novelty in the heart of Tuscany

Meo Modo, the restaurant at Borgo Santo Pietro, can be described in two simple words: "Taste Tuscany." From the passion for sourcing seasonal ingredients, to the search for authentic integrity in simple things such as the bread on the table, to the chef's own foraging in the woods for wild herbs and flowers, there is neither a detail overlooked, nor a nuance neglected. It is all about refinement, not experimentation. Chef Andrea Mattei is a Tuscan, and the things he does – plucking nettle to add to herbal teas or picking wild chicory to add to salads or using wild dandelions as a filling in ravioli or wild asparagus for a frittata – are done because that's what he has always done. Tuscans are connected to the land in the way that fishermen are connected to the sea. They know the bounty on offer because they grew up with it. They know all the wild plants and flowers, which ones you can eat, and which ones have medicinal value. Even the experience of how your food arrives and what it looks like on the table is subject to the same relentless refinement. That's how this restaurant ended up making their own plates: a collaborative effort between a faïence artisan in Florence, Creative Director Jeanette Thottrup and Chef Andrea Mattei. A dark grey plate with a rough edge, for instance, was designed specifically for risotto, and a cream-coloured plate with a raised inner rim was especially created to hold boat-shaped *barchetta* pasta. There are also unexpected touches introduced from Borgo Santo Pietro's own landscape. Large stones dug up from the local riverbed, are ground into serving plates, and slivers of cork from a nearby cork forest are used as serving wedges. Even the Borgo's famous bread, made from stone-ground Verna grain, is served on butter-coloured slabs of marble from a quarry near Siena. Dinner at Meo Modo is a total immersion in the taste, the landscape and the culture of Tuscan cuisine.

www.borgosantopietro.com

86__Dinner in an Alpine Barn

Everyone sits at one long, candlelit table

Not so long ago, cows, goats and sheep lived here during the winter months, among bales of hay. Today, the barn of this 18th-century farmhouse in the French Alps is the setting for an atmospheric dinner experience at The Farmhouse, a unique hotel. The animals are gone, but the rugged architecture of the barn remains, and the space is now dominated by one enormous table that can seat twenty. This is Alpine dining the way it should be. Every night is an event, a celebration that takes most of the day to prepare. It is a feast. The tables are set with massive candelabras dripping with wax – there are more candles than you can count – and the table is completely covered with plates, glasses, jugs, silverware and more, in the manner of a *grande famille* at Christmas. The guests for the evening meet in the living room of The Farmhouse for an aperitif. Dinner is announced the old-fashioned way, with the ringing of a gong, and then everyone moves to the barn, where you are seated, according to a seating plan devised by the staff. The menu is an Alpine *menu du jour*, a collection of dishes for which the French Alps are famous, such as *raclette, fondue* and *tartiflette*. Normally, there are three courses, plus the cheese and salad that comes *à la française* – after the meal. And, of course, there's dessert. Nobody, thankfully, is counting calories, and the prevailing philosophy here is, "Anyway, you've been skiing all day." You do not have to stay at The Farmhouse to have dinner in their barn. Providing there is availability, outside bookings are accepted. So you could be camping in the snow and still be able to partake in one of the most original and delicious dining experiences that exist in the mountains. There's a warmth and a sense of camaraderie to dining in this old barn that no restaurant can match. It's a great adventure and a wonderful reminder that these mountains were here long before skiers discovered them.

___ www.thefarmhouse.fr

87__Picnic at Pont du Gard

Lunch under the world's most important Roman monument

Of all the monuments the ancient Romans left behind, the Pont du Gard is the most magnificent. This bridge is not just a feat of engineering as the tallest of surviving Roman structures – it's a work of extraordinary and timeless beauty! The design has inspired countless architects and builders over the ages. Beyond the poetry of the aesthetics, the monumentality of the scale and the mind-boggling notion that this beautiful structure was built more than 2,000 years ago, there is the equally intriguing question, "Why did 1,000 men toil for five years to build this massive monument?" It was not part of any road or road network, nor was it intended for military or strategic purposes. And the answer was: to carry water, running water, from a stream near Uzès, down to the Roman city of Nemausus (Nîmes). Nothing more! Such complexity and effort to achieve such a simple task distinguishes the Pont du Gard as the supreme example of Ancient Rome at its best. To see this monument in real life is an experience in itself, but it can be much more than that. It can be the setting for the most unusual, exotic and eccentric picnic you've ever had. As you approach the bridge for the first time, watch out for the path that takes you through the trees and down to a pebble beach, where the Gard River takes a small bend. The water is crystal clear and cold, and the massive scale of the Pont Du Gard comes into fresh perspective because you are virtually underneath it. Swimming and a picnic with such a backdrop is surreal, an immersion in history. And it's so easy to do. In the morning, head to Les Halles, the famous covered farmer's market of Avignon to buy bread, cheese, tomatoes, *saucisson*, apricots and peaches. Pack it all in a woven rattan shopping bag that you can also buy at Les Halles, and get in your car for the 20-minute drive that will take you 2,000 years back in time.

www.pontdugard.fr/en/ancient-work-art
www.la-mirande.fr

88__Coffee with Canova

A cappuccino in the former atelier of the sculptor

Italian sculptor Antonio Canova was the Damien Hirst of his day. In the early 19th century, he was the most acclaimed artist in Europe, and he had some of the biggest and best clients, including the Pope, and Napoleon Bonaparte, Emperor of France. In 1802, Canova was commissioned to make a bust of Napoleon, which led to discussions about creating a full statue. And so, Canova made a larger-than-life marble statue, ironically titled *Napoleon as Mars the Peacemaker*. The crated statue arrived in Paris in 1811. But Napoleon was away on the battlefield, and after his defeat at the Battle of Waterloo, the British Government purchased Canova's statue instead and presented it to the victorious Duke of Wellington, who placed it in the stairwell of his stately London home, called Apsley House, where the statue stands to this day. There is a poignantly poetic irony to the idea that the British general who defeated Napoleon would have a giant, naked sculpture of his

nemesis at the bottom of his stairs. Canova went on to make many more masterpieces, and today his work is spread amongst the world's most prestigious museums. But perhaps his most notorious piece stands in the smallest venue: the exquisite Galleria Borghese in Rome. Completed in 1808, *Venus Victrix* is a nude sculpture of Pauline Bonaparte, the sister of Napoleon. Canova had imagined her as Diana, suitably dressed in ancient Roman attire, but Pauline, who was a Borghese by marriage, insisted that the statue be nude. She wanted to be Venus – not Diana. So, now that you know who Canova was, you can understand how special and unusual it is that Canova's former studio on Via del Babuino now operates as a café. At Caffé Canova Tadolini, you are surrounded by all of the neoclassical plaster maquettes (studies) that the artist left behind. Only in Rome will you find a place like this, where you can have your cappuccino with Canova.

—— www.canovatadolini.com

89__ Colonial Brunch in a Paris Tea Warehouse

Indulging in the style of Indochine in the Marais

Tea was one of Europe's first consumable connections with the Orient. When tea first started to become popular in Europe in the mid-17th century, it was an expensive and rare commodity. Around 1660, two brothers from Paris, Pierre and Nicolas Mariage, traveled far to find tea for the king's East India Company. Pierre was sent to Madagascar, and Nicolas made several trips to Persia and India. Thereafter, generation after generation of the Mariage family remained in the tea trade. In 1854, Henri and Édouard Mariage founded the Mariage Frères tea company, importing premium-quality tea to sell wholesale. Then, in 1983, Mariage Frères transformed itself into a retail emporium situated in the original Mariage warehouse on Rue Bourg Tibourg in the part of Paris known as Le Marais. It is no exaggeration to say that this establishment is one of the most exotic, authentic and impressive tea emporiums in the world. Apart from the extraordinary variety of loose leaf tea available and the sheer number of unusual teapots for sale, the real draw of this fascinating emporium is the restaurant at the back. The Mariage Frères tea warehouse restaurant provides a culinary window into the colonial days of Indochine. The waiters are clad in elegant Nehru jackets with rows and rows of polished brass buttons, the furniture is a blend of rattan and antiques, and the food has a recurrent theme of… tea. Dishes include guacamole seasoned with matcha green tea powder, houmous infused with Zen fruit tea, mesclun seasoned with Marco Polo tea, and "Tahitian-style" sea bass infused with Hawaiian Kawaii tea. For brunch, which is definitely a must, you have to try Le Classique, a beautifully arranged bento box that includes toasted brioche, *gelées extra de thé* (tea jelly), scrambled eggs seasoned with matcha, artisan smoked salmon, Japanese matcha *fromage frais*, and a champagne cocktail prepared with the very rare and elusive Russian white tea.

www.mariagefreres.com/UK/ restaurant_and_tea_salon_le_marais_ bourg_tibourg.html

ORIGINAL CYCLING

Cycling is a brilliant way to explore. It will open your eyes and stimulate your senses, not to mention the fact that it's good for your health. And I'm not the only one who is enthusiastic about cycling adventures. An entire industry has sprung up around cycling all over the world as an alternative, "slower" way to explore. The cycling adventures listed in this chapter are by no means comprehensive or inclusive. I would need an entire book for that. They are merely a taste of what can be experienced on two wheels. What these cycling adventures have in common is that they are quite unexpected, quite unusual and quite surprising. In other words... they are original!

cycling on ile de ré ●
cycling the côte sauvage ●

● *cycling to the beach in venice*
● *cycling around florence*

cycling the rice fields of ubud

90__Cycling the Rice Fields of Ubud

Narrow trails lead through Bali's verdant beauty

Ubud, in the highlands of Bali, is an imposing and magical landscape of dense tropical rainforest and sculptured terraces of rice paddies, dotted with Hindu temples and holy shrines. It is also the island's centre for authentic handcraft and traditional dance. No wonder it is known as the spiritual heart of "the island of the gods." Of all the rice fields in the world, some of the most spectacular are in Ubud. These centuries-old terraces of verdant green, arranged like giant Escher drawings, are so special that many are protected as UNESCO Heritage sites. There are two ways to experience these geometric spectacles of nature. You can park yourself in a chair at a restaurant that looks out on these famous rice terraces, or you can make them the focus of a genuine adventure in the saddle of a mountain bike. The most magnificent rice fields of Ubud are more remote and unspoilt, and they are only accessible by narrow paths created by the farmers to access their fields that are also just wide enough to accommodate a scooter or a bicycle. The steep and undulating terrain is well-suited for mountain bikes or electric mountain bikes, depending on how sporty you are. This is an adventure in an exotic location that offers a genuine slice of Bali. It is intrepid and unusual, but also perfectly safe to embark on as a family adventure. Logistically, it is relatively straightforward to organize and arrange because there are many garages and shops on the outskirts of Ubud that rent all the equipment you could need, and they also offer guides who know how to access the parts you would otherwise not find on your own. So leave the touristy restaurants to people happy to sit on their asses, and put your own ass on the saddle of a mountain bike and disappear into a fantasy world of monumental, organic, green terraces.

— www.ebikesbali.com

91__Cycling on Île de Ré

Bike paths criss-cross a charmingly French island

Famous for its salt marshes and fishing villages, Île de Ré is the perfect island for cycling. The terrain is flat, and there are plenty of bike paths that snake their way through the scenery. There's really not much to Île de Ré though. It is a small, flat island with salt marshes, sand dunes, beaches and cycle paths, and its fishing villages have changed little over the centuries. You can count the old ports on one hand. There's St-Martin, La Flotte, Ars-en-Ré, and Les Portes, and none have high-rise hotels, apartment buildings, marinas or shopping centres. It is as it has always been, a tiny island in the Atlantic Ocean with a handful of beaches and fishing villages. And that's exactly what makes it one of the most popular summer destinations for the French, especially Parisians. The urban crowd loves this kind of authenticity and rusticity, and they are willing to pay for it. A small fisherman's cottage in Ars-en-Ré, for instance, is not cheap. Many city dwellers are drawn to the primal simplicity that Île de Ré offers. A typical day consists of going to the beach or biking through the dunes, all planned around lunch and dinner. Food plays a big role, and the fact that all the towns have weekly farmers' markets is no coincidence. The temporary residents from Paris wouldn't have it any other way. In the summer months, there's a rhythm to life on Île de Ré that is addictively uncomplicated – a combination of a healthy lifestyle and wholesome food with none of the over-the-top nightlife you would normally expect from an exclusive resort town. Pretty much everyone who comes to Île de Ré stays in renovated fishing cottages, and it is almost a badge of honor to see who can live the most simply. A cycling adventure here is easy. All you need is a map of the island's bike paths and an itinerary of where you want to go. You can rent a house and use it as your base, or cycle to different ports, where each town has at least one irresistible boutique hotel.

__ www.hotel-le-senechal.com

92__Cycling the Côte Sauvage

Two wheels to explore the Quiberon Peninsula

The Quiberon Peninsula is a splendid and unspoilt slice of Brittany. All the best and most dramatic attributes of Bretagne - the beaches, the coves, the cliffs, the dunes and the salt-of-the-earth fishing villages - are here, crammed onto a 14-kilometre-long peninsula jutting out into the Atlantic. For hundreds of years, this area was home to a serious fishing community and once boasted the leading sardine port in France. The men would go out to sea, while the women worked in the sardine factories. There are still a few canneries left, but the last century has seen a gradual shift from fishing to tourism. Of all the places in Brittany, the Quiberon peninsula surely ranks as the best and most rewarding location for a cycling tour. If you do it without stopping, the Tour de Quiberon will take two and a half hours, but there's not much sense in that. You should make the most of it and take a full day to do it properly. Part of the appeal of this peninsula is the way the landscape changes from the sandy beaches and calm bays of the east coast (which are so well suited to the cultivation of oysters), to the jagged cliffs and dunes of the west coast. My favourite part is a stretch of the west coast known as the Côte Sauvage (the Savage Coast), a collection of small bays, dramatic cliffs, and natural stone arches carved by the unrelenting pounding of the Atlantic surf. Despite the attractive hue of the turquoise waters, it is forbidden to swim along this part of the west coast because of strong rip tides and currents, but boogie boarding and surfboards are allowed because their boards qualify as flotation devices. The gateway for this adventure is the mainland town of Plouharnel. Here, you can hire bikes at Les Vélos de la Baie if you don't have your own, and before you head out, you should definitely eat a crêpe or two at La Clef de la Presqu'île at 15 Avenue de l'Ocean. A more authentically-French cycling adventure does not exist.

___ www.cyclesloisirs.com/location

93__Cycling around Florence

Avoid the crowds by cycling along the River Arno

The best way to enjoy Florence without getting caught in a tourist trap is to cycle your way around town. Birthplace of the Renaissance, this famous city has been investing in alternative travel for the past few years, which includes building a substantial cycle route along the River Arno. This is a proper and separate road for cyclists that runs along the length of the Arno's path through the historic city of Florence. Apart from the stunning and unique vista it offers as you glide along the river towards the Ponte Vecchio, the route also takes you away from the congestion of the inner-city centre. To experience Florence at its best, head out early, while most tourists are still having breakfast. Alternatively, opt for a lazy start and cycle into town just before lunch. The cycle path goes straight past Il Borro Tuscan Bistro, which answers the question of where to have lunch without feeling like a tourist. There is no better or more authentic place in Florence for Tuscan food. After lunch, cross the

bridge in front of Il Borro and head to the neighborhood known as the Oltrarno, which is the decidedly less touristy and more authentic part of town. It has plenty of hidden piazzas, cafés and shops, including Giulio Giannini e Figlio, established in 1856, which makes the most exquisite stationery and notebooks. When the sun starts to go down, make your way back across the Arno, park your bike in the small courtyard of the all-white Hotel Continentale and head for the lifts. Go to the top floor, and you will emerge onto the best rooftop bar in Florence. This is more than a bar – it's a platform from which to admire the historic centre, including the Ponte Vecchio, which lies directly below. Then, when most visitors start to return to their hotels or head out to dinner, it's time to get back on your bike and cycle around the Duomo, the cathedral that launched the Renaissance, as a fun and interesting way to grasp the scale and exquisite decorative detail of this architectural masterpiece.

—— www.rivalofts.com

94__Cycling to the Beach in Venice

Do something different in Venice: go to the beach

Who even knew Venice had a beach? But it does, and it's a lot bigger and sandier than you would expect. It could and should be a part of your Venice adventure. Going to the beach is certainly a brilliant way to get away from the crowds and the heat, and it's surprisingly easy to get to. All you need is a water taxi. Just mention the word "Lido" to the driver, and he will take you straight across the lagoon - a 15-minute journey - to a pier on Lido island, from which it is no more than a 15-minute walk to the beach. The beach is a huge, broad stretch of pale sand that goes on uninterrupted for many kilometres. Better still, the only people on it are Italians on holiday, and not even that many, even in peak season. Behind the beach, Lido island faces back across the lagoon at Venice from the shade of plenty of mature plane trees, and the noise from the cicadas chirping away is a welcome change from the hustle and bustle of the city. The Lido is a

world away from touristy Venice, and the best way to explore this beach island is on a bicycle. With a bike, you can discover the little bakeries, trattorias and pizza places hidden away on this lush, low-key island. Your bicycle helps you to choose the end of the beach that you prefer because the beach goes on for quite a distance. If you ride your bike around Lido, you will also likely stumble across the very white and very modern architectural complex called the Palazzo del Cinema, purpose-built in 1937 for the Venice Film Festival, the world's oldest. You will also no doubt cycle past the historic Hotel Excelsior on the beach, the scene of many a celebrity reception during the film festival each year. My advice is to "reverse-engineer" your Venice experience. Why not stay in a beautiful (and much cheaper) hotel on Lido island, a stone's throw from the beach, and make your way to Venice by water taxi whenever you want?

___ www.hotelexcelsiorvenezia.com

UNREAL ESTATE

Scattered haphazardly around the world, there are some buildings that are so unusual, so unique, and so completely charming that they constitute an adventure in their own right. Some are handmade, some are concrete, some are new… and some are as old as time itself. What they all have in common is that simply staying "overnight" becomes an adventure you will never forget.

hippo treehouse

mix the contents of an austrian "schloss" with a mining camp.

the beauty of mexico's coast and the beauty of mexico's colours

teepee motel

arctic igloo

tivoli gardens pavillion

american treehouse

normandy chateau

camping in paris

frontier ghost town

tee pee motel

cassis winery

venice boathouse

the tumbling town

prehistoric caves

sardinia lighthouse

maharaja's stables

sumba stone shack

hippo tree house

franschhoek vineyard

hermanus surf shack

95__Hippo Tree House

In a tree above a pond filled with Hippopotamuses

I have stayed at many safari lodges. Some are very architectural, some are very stylish and some are both. But none constitute an adventure like the Hippo Tree House at Ulusaba, in South Africa's Sabi Sands. This thatched-roof structure, suspended high on a bunch of cross-braced telegraph poles, sits above the shore of a small pond populated by dozens of hippopotamuses. At night, these huge beasts sleep directly beneath the treehouse. They even rub against the timber support poles occasionally, and you can feel, ever so slightly, the treehouse swaying as a result. As you may have heard, hippos are incredibly dangerous. They look cute and chubby, laid back and harmless, but they are immensely powerful and merciless killers – even a crocodile is no match for a hippo. Thus, there's no way that you can set foot on the ground anywhere near the treehouse, and therein lies another unique part of the adventure. To access the rest of the lodge, like the pavilion that houses the restaurant, the tree house is connected via a series of suspension bridges that wind through the surrounding canopy of trees. Thus, you make your way to breakfast like Tarzan, and you are already one adventure up on the other sleepy-eyed guests.

____ www.sabi-sands.com/ulusaba-safari-lodge.php

A safari is one thing – staying in a treehouse above a hippopotamus pond, on safari, is another. It's an adventure within an adventure. At night, the treehouse sways gently back and forth from hippos scratching themselves against the treehouse's support structure. It's too dangerous to be near the ground, so the path to breakfast is via suspension bridges. If you happen to encounter a leopard lounging on a branch along the way, consider it an adventure bonus.

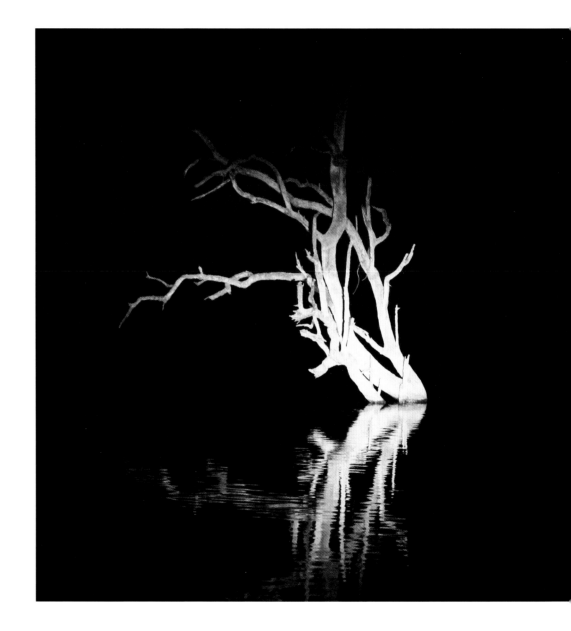

96__Frontier Ghost Town

An old silver-mining camp reinvented as a retreat

True story: there's a ghost town in the Rocky Mountains of Colorado at an altitude of 3,000+ metres. Dunton Hot Springs is in the San Juan Ranges, a two-hour drive from the town of Durango, which used to be the hideout of the real Butch Cassidy and his Hole-in-the-Wall Gang. All the names are there, crudely carved for all to see, in the wooden counter of the old silver mining town's saloon bar. In the late 1800s and early 1900s, this was a silver mining camp, populated by hopeful prospectors who built various cabins and structures, the dance hall and the saloon bar being the most elaborate. But then, like many mining towns in the Rockies, the silver dried up, and the tiny town eventually became a "ghost town." And then two gentlemen involved in the world of film producing made the trip out to this wild and remote corner of Colorado and decided to buy the whole town. They had a plan, and it was certainly not to go "all fancy." In fact, Christoph Henkel and Bernt Kuhlmann were intent on preserving the distinct, forlorn patina and rugged ambience of this "make-do" mining camp, and they made the inspired decision to fix up every other cabin, leaving quite a few derelict, and making sure that the "mod cons" for the ones that were renovated (on the inside) were duly buried under the ground. The result is something quite special - a genuine prospector's town from the Wild West of the 19th century, which still looks and feels like a mining camp, just as it would have when Butch Cassidy and his gang first rode into town to hide out after robbing the bank in nearby Telluride.

www.duntondestinations.com/hot-springs

Place the contents from an old schloss (castle) in Austria into an abandoned mining camp high in the Rocky Mountains of Colorado, and you start to understand the magic of Dunton Hot Springs. Family hunting trophies, bear rugs, antique chairs, irreplaceable tapestries and old world maps, globes and books constitute the unlikely interiors of these dilapidated wooden shacks. Surrounded by pristine, untouched wilderness, Dunton is a fairy-tale adventure of unexpected contrasts.

97__Sumba Stone Shack

*A modern limestone villa set amongst the raw and
rugged beauty of a primordial island*

The Indonesian island of Sumba is the closest you will get on this planet to a real-life Jurassic Park. It is green… overwhelmingly green! There are waterfalls everywhere and muddy rivers and plenty of water buffalo and dense jungle that rolls with the hilly landscape down to huge empty beaches. Not only do Sumba's beaches make Australian beaches look small, but they also host surprisingly turquoise waters, big waves and wild horses. You half expect an extinct species to come roaring out of the forest because this is one of the few places on the planet that has hardly experienced "civilisation" as we know it. There are no cities, or towns… no apartment buildings, no hotels, no restaurants, no stores, no shops, no supermarkets, no cafés… none. It is primitive in the most beautiful sense. Nature, not humans, still rules here. So it is probably the last place you expect to find a beautiful modern limestone villa with amazing views and a gorgeous swimming pool. Yet here it is, 100 yards from one of the best surf beaches on the island. How it

got here is legend. An Australian couple, he, a builder, she, an architect, were on vacation when they got a call from an excited friend. "Sumba is unbelievable. You guys have to build a place here," he told them. "But we're travelling in Europe," they responded. "Doesn't matter," the friend replied. "I'll buy it for you." And he did – a plot big enough for a substantial six-bedroom property plus garden. When the intrepid owners of this newly-acquired beach-front land finally arrived on the island, they quickly learned that an island with no building has no builders. Undeterred, they took on 120 locals and taught them how to work with stone, wood and metal, while the couple patiently parked themselves in a bamboo shack on the beach, for two years. It's an extraordinary story, but the result is even more so. Alamayah is a sophisticated and stylish boutique hotel built entirely in the local limestone, smack bang in the middle of a prehistoric setting, less than a two-hour drive from Sumba's Tambolaka airport.

_____ www.alamayah.com

The genius of this hideaway on Sumba's idyllic coast is its combination of a thoroughly wild and remote setting with the unexpected luxury and lifestyle of a stunning modern villa built in stone. This is the very definition of a Tropical Dream: authentic, exotic, splendid and… wild.

98__Venice Boathouse

Watching Venice float by from an old boathouse

Venice is tricky. It can be magical, or it can be awful. Now that it is cheaper to fly there for a weekend than to stay in London, it has become a challenge to enjoy this extraordinary city. As a destination, it is still mesmerisingly beautiful and uniquely exotic, but it also attracts a lot of visitors. The trick, thus, is to avoid the tourist traps and to avoid feeling like a tourist. You want to keep it authentic – as authentic as possible – and that not only applies to where you eat but also to where you stay. The ultimate goal is to stay somewhere so Venetian that even one night ranks as an adventure in its own right. There are not many places that fit this bill – they are rare and difficult to find. But one of the most precious gems I have found, after many, many visits to Venice, is the Charming House iQs. You stay in a very stylish apartment with a bedroom, bathroom and kitchen in a historic mansion on a canal. But best of all, you get a boathouse too. This boathouse, filled with the seawater of Venice's lagoon on a small, private canal, has been converted into a communal living room. So all you need to do is sit on the steps that lead to the water with your morning coffee and watch Venice float by. Tourists in gondolas will stare with intrigue inside your boathouse only to find you, with your coffee, staring right back at them. Your stay in Venice will be transformed into a genuinely personal panorama, a window into the real Venice. And more importantly, you will feel like a Venetian rather than a tourist.

—— www.thecharminghouse.com

99__Cassis Winery

The beauty and romance of a secret side of the Cote D'Azur

Cassis is the Côte d'Azur the way it used to be: small, scenic and pristine. It is a tiny fishing port that still looks like a fishing port, with pastel-coloured houses and quaint cafés lining the quay instead of super yachts. Perhaps the most striking feature is that the craggy peaks of the Alps boldly march their way into the azure blue Mediterranean, enveloping Cassis with their rugged beauty. Nestled snugly in the folds of these same mountains, within walking distance of the port, are picturesque vineyards famous for their rosé wines, in particular the label called Bandol. One of these idyllic vineyards, the one in the most picturesque location and with the most commanding view of all of Cassis, does not make wine anymore. That's because it was transformed by Cynthia Kayser-Maus into a luxurious bed and breakfast. Maison°9 has only four rooms, but these rooms, which are really suites or apartments, all have their own well-equipped kitchen, a beautiful

spacious bathroom and a private terrace. You won't be using the kitchen for anything other than making coffee or tea – why think about cooking when you can stroll down the road and eat in restaurants that serve fish straight off the boats? The adventure of Cassis is personified by Maison°9. Nestled in the surrounding folds of the Alps, it has extraordinary views and a fabulous pool. It is irresistibly romantic, surrounded by wineries, and the four guest suites are more instagrammable than anything in the South of France. No wonder guests are loath to leave the premises. The Côte d'Azur starts in Cassis. No other place on the French Riviera can match Cassis for charm, spectacle, beauty and authenticity. And I'm not the only one to say so. Nobel Prize-winning author Frédéric Mistral put the same sentiments in writing, as did Sir Winston Churchill. A recent post from Vogue read, "This tiny town in the South of France trumps Saint-Tropez any day!"

__ www.maison9.net

100__Wigwam Motel

Get your kicks in a teepee on Route 66

Ever since 1946, when Nat King Cole immortalized in song this highway that takes you through eight states, from Illinois to California, Route 66 has become synonymous with the "American road trip." To be honest, it's not what it used to be, which is both good and bad. If you prefer your Americana à la David Lynch – slightly sleazy and a bit down-and-out – then you will love it. If not, then keep driving. I quite like the fact that Route 66 has been abandoned in favor of the larger, faster Interstate 405. Route 66 is now a defunct, faded version of what it once was, and to be honest, that makes it much more of a genuine adventure. Just after you hit Arizona, there's a place absolutely worth stopping at for a night. The Wigwam Motel is so bizarre that it could have been purpose built by Mr Lynch himself for one of his films. Never will you tire of telling your friends about the night you spent in a concrete wigwam on Route 66. Is it faded? Yes. Has it seen better days? Absolutely. All the more reason to go.

___ www.wigwammotel.com

101__Normandy Château

Bewitched by the beauty of an 800-year-old castle

Château de Canisy is one of the few castles in France that remain intact. This stately palace has been in the Kergorlay family for a thousand years. In 1066, Hugues de Carbonnel, Lord of Canisy, travelled with William, Duke of Normandy, aka William the Conqueror, to fight by his side in the Norman Conquest of England. The château is a place of extraordinary history, impeccable pedigree and stunning architecture. Most importantly, Hugues de Carbonnel de Canisy has managed to retain its 324 hectares of land and to open its doors to paying guests without becoming a hotel. This château is still a château, with more than fifty bedrooms, a music room with harps and harpsichords, a billiard room, a lake with black swans and formal and informal gardens. Château de Canisy is the real thing. When you stay as a paying guest, you are afforded the same privileges as the family that owns it. You can choose to eat in the formal dining room with its immense, 17th-century paintings that glorify the hunt. Or, if it's just the two of you, lunch or dinner can be served in the cosier oval-shaped music room with its beautiful fireplace and splendid views of the lake. You can play croquet on the croquet lawns, fish in the lake or go for an early morning run around the vast estate, when the grey mist of dawn is as thick as pea soup. Château de Canisy is in the heart of Normandy, with the famous D-Day beaches of Omaha and Utah nearby, as well as Mont Saint-Michel, one of the most visited monuments in France. Then, of course, there is your room, which is more like a royal apartment. Packed with history and bubbling over with authentic style, the guest suites are decorated with antiques, and the fabrics and wallpapers are recreated from historical archives. Château de Canisy provides an adventure best summed up as a luxurious step back in time.

____ www.chateaudecanisy.com

102__Prehistoric Caves

Experiencing the Stone Age authenticity of Matera

Humans have been living here since they first started painting the walls of the caves. Matera, the city carved from a canyon in Italy's southern Basilicata, has been a place of residence since the dawn of time. In the 1950s, the conditions in Matera were the shame of Italy. People were living here with their animals; infant mortality was the highest in all of Europe and diseases such as tuberculosis were rife. Life expectancy, not surprisingly, was amongst the lowest in the world. So the Italian Government, embarrassed by this scenario, decided to do something about it. The remaining few who had not emigrated to the United States were given a new town on the other side of the mountain.

Their caves were abandoned and remained so until the squalid ghost town started slowly being rehabilitated a decade and a half ago. Today, Matera, the old Matera, the town that was once a terrible place to live, has become one of the new "must see" destinations in Italy. Visiting Matera is one thing – spending a few nights in a cave is another. It's an adventure that connects you to where we come from – a profoundly primordial experience you will never forget, all made possible by the genius that is Grotte Della Civita. The accommodations are genuine caves that have cleverly transformed into splendid spaces without betraying their crude and utilitarian roots.

www.sextantio.it/en/
legrottedellacivita/matera

103__Sardinia Lighthouse

Isolated bliss in a remote corner of Sardinia

To get to this extraordinary lighthouse perched on a rocky promontory on the Southern tip of Sardinia, just keep driving south until the road ends. Only then does it get more complicated. The only way you will get to this lighthouse is if you're an officer of the Italian Navy or a lucky guest at Faro Capo Spartivento. Courtesy of maritime regulations regarding the security of lighthouses, Faro Capo Spartivento is as exclusive and private as it gets. In the entire lexicon of "recycled real estate," this property must be one of the most unusual ones ever to be converted into a hotel. Built in 1854 at the command of Victor Emmanuel II. It hosted a lighthouse keeper until 1980, when the operation became automated. By the time that Capo Faro Spartivento attracted the attention of a local property developer in 2006, the lighthouse had deteriorated significantly. But four years of fastidious work transformed the once sober and utilitarian building into an elegant and highly unusual hideaway. Outside, it still looks the same. Inside, it's a design dream. It helps, of course that the proprietor, Alessio Raggio, is someone *The New York Times* refers to as "the Andre Balazs of Southern Sardinia." A Lighthouse is limited for space, so it was never going to be a big hotel, a restriction that Raggio has used to his advantage. He decided he might as well go upmarket. That's why this lighthouse has a glass-sided horizon pool cantilevered from the rocky cliffs. And that's why the roof – a 2,500-square-foot (250-square-metre) space with extraordinary views – has elegant daybeds for sunbathing and enjoying the sunset. And that's why the six suites are white and modern and equipped with every convenience, including beautifully-designed bathrooms. But the real *ne plus ultra* is the location. Surrounded by sandy beaches, this lighthouse is for travellers who take their hedonism seriously. Is it expensive? Hell yeah! But I would rather be here for two nights than somewhere mediocre for a week.

www.farocapospartivento.com

Nestled into the rugged boulders that define the southernmost tip of Sardinia, this converted lighthouse offers something that is increasingly difficult to find in Europe. Namely, the luxury of complete privacy, peace and solitude, in an exceptionally beautiful setting.

104__Tivoli Gardens Pavilion

Sleeping in the amusement park that inspired Walt Disney

Nimb Hotel is not something you will find anywhere else in the world. It is an extraordinary boutique hotel inside the exotic "make believe" Oriental Palace, within the world's oldest amusement park in the centre of Denmark's capital city. Tivoli Gardens first opened in Copenhagen in 1843. King Christian VIII of Denmark allowed the six hectares in what is now the city centre to be developed as an amusement park because the founder, George Carstensen, had convinced the king, saying, "People who are amusing themselves do not think about politics." Ultimately, Tivoli proved such an enduring success that it even served as the inspiration for Walt Disney's Disneyland. Amazingly, the wooden roller coaster built in 1914 is still one of the most enduring attractions, as is the Moorish-inspired Dancehall Palace, built in 1909. Danish television even broadcasted weekend dance programs filmed at this palace, which looks like something out of 1001 Arabian Nights. Today, the same fantasy has been converted beautifully into a hotel with all the bells and whistles. Design-wise, it's what you would expect from the land that gave us "Scandi-Chic." In the case of Nimb, it's Scandi-Chic with an Oriental twist. There's a pool on the roof, a spa and a gym in the basement, a charming café, an assortment of restaurants facing the park and a collection of guest suites with fireplaces, balconies and terraces. And yet, the defining characteristic, the one unique quality that stands out above and beyond all the others, is the fact that because you are inside Tivoli Gardens, the only thing you need to do to access all the rides is simply to turn the doorknob and walk outside. Nimb guests get a special armband that entitles you to all rides and activities for the entirety of your stay. Surely, this must rank as the most desirable adventure destination for any kid – of any age.

___ www.nimb.dk

105__Hermanus Surf Shack

Sperm whales and crashing surf for breakfast

Not many beach shacks feature sperm whales launching themselves into the air. It is not guaranteed you would witness this extraordinary mating ritual, as it depends on the time of the year, but you have more chances here on the breakfast deck of Birkenhead House than most other places in the world. I was lucky. A massive mature whale breached the water while I was having breakfast, and I will never forget it. It was a rare privilege and one that very few people will witness. Yet, extraordinarily, a sperm whale breaching the ocean surface just in front of you is not the adventure on offer – it's a bonus. Even if you don't see the whales, you might stumble onto what must be the most perfect beach shack in the world. It is located on the rocks at the edge of the ocean in the coastal town of Hermanus. And at this gourmet destination, the food stacks up to anything you might be served in fancier restaurants in California. With its perfect service, this is the only beach shack I know of where the staff outnumber the guests. Everything, from crystal decanters filled with local mineral water to the Chinese antiques in every room, seems to have been carefully considered. The personal service is phenomenal. Whatever you may ask for, they will get it for you in a jiffy. And yet it still feels like a beach house – and that's because it was a beach house until the children grew up and it was too big for the couple who own it. So they changed it just enough to accommodate paying guests. That's the secret. It is not a hotel designed to look like a beach house; it's a beach house that now functions as a hotel. Watch whales, walk on the beach, swim, surf or do nothing. That's the adventure of the beach shack.

www.theroyalportfolio.com/birkenhead-house/overview

Hermanus is the African beach we dream about. A rugged and imposing crescent of pale sand and blue water. No wonder sperm whales come here to mate. Birkenhead House is the ultimate Hermanus surf shack, built on the edge of this famous beach, like an observatory for watching whales.

106__Maharaja's Stables

Glamping in the former stables of the Thakur of Samode

Rajasthan is the India we all want to visit – the India of turbans, tigers, palaces, elephants and maharajas. The famous triangle of Jaipur, Jodhpur and Udaipur has captured collective imagination for hundreds of years with dashing tales of tiger hunts and polo played on elephants. Mughal invaders were responsible for the majesty we now associate with Rajasthan. They were there for hundreds of years. And it is here that the Mughal conquerors achieved the pinnacle of their culture, a legacy that may have faded over the past centuries but not to the point that there is nothing left to marvel at. Like peacocks in the wild, there are still poignant remnants of the spectacle and experiences that inspired artists and writers alike. You just have to know where to

look. Samode Bagh, for example, is the former stables of the Thakur of Samode. It is neither minimal nor modern. This expanse of green, with its extensive lawns and mature trees, was once the training ground and stables of the horses belonging to the Royal Family of Samode. Stallions of noble descent were exercised, paraded and bathed here. Strangely, this same venue works extremely well today for a maharaja-style version of "glamping." Instead of stables, there are now tents. And the green lands that once would have exercised the Royal Cavalry are now used as a setting for high tea. With swimming pools of exquisite decoration and tents that feature study areas and bathrooms, Samode Bagh has given a new regal twist to camping in Rajasthan.

__ www.samode.com/samodebagh

107__Avatar Treehouse

A magic world on the Island of the Gods

Truth be told, I don't remember much about the film *Avatar*. But I do remember the houses. Suspended, on stilts, in idyllic stretches of jungle, peering into misty, surreal ravines, they remain… memorably exotic. I'm not sure whether the film was inspiration for this property, built on the edge of a spectacular waterfall in Bali, but it certainly shares the same exotic signature. If you can find it, that is. Nirjhara is the very definition of a hidden gem. Situated not far from the famous temple of Tanah Lot, it is the first "high end" establishment to be built near Kedungu Beach. Surfers know this spot and are very reluctant to share it, which explains why most people have never heard of it. It is the very definition of unspoilt Bali. The beach is big and empty, with a famous reef break beloved by surfers. The surrounding landscape consists of verdant green, undulating rice fields and patches of jungle near rivers that run from the mountains to the sea. A three-story-high waterfall is the last thing you expect to find so close to the beach, and this makes the Avatar treehouses even more spectacular. The crashing water is the dominant view from the bedrooms, and you will occasionally spot the odd giant lizard (same family as the Komodo Dragon) sunbathing in the shallows near the falls. Add a private cinema, a large, saltwater horizon pool underneath the waterfall and a restaurant with the perfect view of the tumbling cascade, and you start to get an idea of what makes these eight Avatar treehouses so special. The setting, the location and the view ensure you do not need to leave your treehouse to be entertained. But it would be a shame because there is world-class surfing nearby, horses to ride on the black sand beaches that continue all the way up the coast, and mountain bikes to use to explore the villages and surroundings.

__ www.cedarcreektreehouse.com

This place is not what you would ever expect to find near the beach in Bali. The most surprising feature is the view of a spectacular three-story waterfall situated just below your futuristic tropical treehouse. You feel like you are immersed in the famous jungles of Bali's volcanic peaks, but, in fact, you are so near the beach that the ocean is easily visible from your rooftop observation deck. It takes less than five minutes to cycle to nearby Kedungu Beach, which happens to be known as one of the best surf spots on Bali's west coast.

108__Franschhoek Vineyard

The charm and beauty of South Africa's vineyards

Cape Town is surrounded by wine country. There are the vineyards of Groot Constantia, Stellenbosch and, the prettiest of them all, Franschhoek. These are not new vineyards – the wine regions in Cape Town have been there since the late 1600s. Of all the vineyards in the world, it's hard to imagine an area that combines history and natural beauty and monumental landscape as convincingly as Franschhoek. Plus, it has a fascinating story. When the Dutch – via their corporation, the VOC, announced their plan to dominate the world's spice trade, they didn't just need ships and crews – they needed something their merchant seamen could drink without getting sick. Bottled wine was the most practical solution, and so they enticed the French Huguenot refugees, who had been kicked out of France by Louis XIV because of their religious beliefs, to start a new life as wine growers in the Cape Town regions of South Africa. The arrangement was simple. The recently-arrived. Huguenot farmers would receive land, tools, building materials and seeds – in short everything they needed to create vineyards. The farmers, in turn, would set aside a certain number of bottles of wine for the VOC crew. Thus, a clever and efficient codependency helped create one of the most charming and beautiful wine regions in the world. Nestled in the fold of the Drakenstein Mountains, surrounded by imposing peaks and cliffs, Franschhoek successfully mixes the French reputation for making wine with the architecture of the Cape Dutch, and the magnificent charisma of South Africa's southern coastline. The adventure on offer here is the unapologetic life of a hedonist, especially if you are lucky enough to stay at La Residence Hotel Villas. Situated in the middle of its own vineyard, flanked by the stony cliffs of the surrounding mountains, La Residence combines Cape Dutch proportions with Chinese antiques, Persian rugs and fireplaces. It is one of the most romantic places in all of Africa. Just being here is the adventure.

www.theroyalportfolio.com/la-residence/overview

109__Arctic Igloo

Living in a palace made entirely of ice

Every year, it melts in the spring, and every year in the autumn, they build it again from scratch. It is never the same twice. The Ice Hotel in Jukkasjärvi, Sweden is more than a crazy place to stay. It's an art installation in the frozen North that you can sleep in. Is it comfortable? No, not in the classic five star sense! But it is definitely an adventure – a worthwhile adventure – a very memorable adventure. And not just because your bedroom is in an igloo built entirely out of ice. The Ice Hotel organises outdoor expeditions, such as snow-mobile safaris, that explore the surprisingly colourful buildings of the Sami, the native dwellers of this habitat 200 km north of the Arctic Circle. Local churches and houses are painted bright shades of yellow, green, red and blue, as if you were in the Caribbean. Then there's the Ice Hotel's church, built entirely out of frozen water – beautiful and serene, like something out of science fiction – that has become very popular for

weddings, even with locals. And, of course, there is the Ice Bar, a place where multi-colored vodka shots are served in fist-sized blocks of ice, whilst the "ambient" temperature remains a constant -7°C. A palace made of ice is a fabulous fantasy all by itself, but the Ice Hotel is also a testament to a sophisticated sense of architecture and design. Frozen water, per se, does not have any structural strength. The ice that is used to build the Ice Hotel is cut from a nearby river because a flowing river that freezes creates ice that is formed under pressure, and this ice has strength similar to concrete. At the Ice Hotel, science meets art. Even one night here is an experience you are not likely to forget. There is no electricity, so your room is illuminated with dozens of beeswax candles. To be able to survive the Arctic cold, you are issued an Arctic-graded sleeping bag. There is no place on the planet more unusual and more original than this giant igloo in Sweden's frozen North.

___ www.icehotel.com

110__ The Tumbling Town

The unique theatre of Italy's most captivating town

It is a scene from *The Lord of the Rings*: a tiny medieval town perched on a mountain-top, with sheer drops on all sides. The only way to get to it is via a steep, vertigo-inducing footbridge that crosses the ravine and separates the town from the rest of the world. This isolated, exposed peak hardly looks large enough to support a town that currently includes a piazza, a church, some cafés, a bar, a few trattorias and a dozen or so houses. Every once in a while, a chunk of rock breaks off and tumbles into the abyss, taking a building with it. Erosion, over time, is gradually and literally making the town smaller. Civita di Bagnoregio is known and loved by Italians, as *la citta che muore* ("the dying town"), and it has inspired poets and writers alike. In the words of Bonaventura Tecchi, "I would never have become a writer if I had not lived for a few months every year, from July to November, in the valley of Civita, with its vision of the white crests, the golden volcanic clay, and the eloquent ruins of the city that is dying…." Civita di Bagnoregio has quite a history. It was founded by the Etruscans 2,500 years ago and was the birthplace of Saint Bonaventure, although the house where he was born has long since fallen away. Despite its diminutive size, Civita has played a major role for the Catholic Church, almost since the beginning. There has been a bishop of Civita di Bagnoregio, for instance, since around A.D. 600. That's how such a tiny town ended up with such an imposing church. It even qualified as a cathedral until earthquake damage justified building a newer cathedral in a nearby town in the late 1600s. Just behind the church is the bishop's former residence, and behind that is a former school for training priests that is now operated as a bed-and-breakfast. It is, appropriately, called Corte della Maestà ("Court of Majesty"), which encapsulates the Tumbling Town experience, perfectly.

____ www.cortedellamaesta.com

111__Camping in Paris

Along the river, under the trees, a Parisian surprise

Tucked away in a corner of the Bois de Boulogne, on the banks of the Seine, there is a campsite called Camping de Paris. With its unexpectedly bucolic country setting, it gives the impression that Paris is many miles away. Yet, if you jump on a bike, it takes no more than 15 minutes to cycle to the Eiffel Tower. Camping in Paris? The words don't sound like they belong in the same sentence. Given the historic avenues and charming little streets in the city centre, it is difficult to imagine that camping is a possibility. And that's exactly what makes it such a wonderful experience. Best of all, you don't need your own tent or caravan. Camping de Paris has free-standing bungalows and wooden gypsy caravans, or *roulottes*, fitted out to accommodate small families, that can be rented on a nightly or weekly basis. The campground also has a tiny grocery store, a small café and a wood-fired pizza oven. But the big draw of camping in Paris

is Mother Nature. If you are intrigued by the possibility of combining urban excursions into Paris – to sample the croissants of the city's *boulangeries*, the cakes and pastries of the *pâtisseries*, and the *menu du jour* offered by the *brasseries* – with outdoor activities in the Bois de Boulogne, then this is an experience well worth considering. The Bois de Boulogne is the lungs of Paris. This forested park is full of fountains, lakes and bike tracks, and Parisian parents head here on weekends with their children. If you are camping, it becomes your base, as well as your daily route to the city, and the beating heart of Paris is only a 15-minute bike ride away. For anyone skeptical about cycling in Paris, things have recently changed a lot. The roads that once ran right beside the Seine have now been reinvented as cycling and pedestrian paths. You can use them to access most of inner-city Paris without getting caught up in dangerous traffic.

—— www.campingparis.fr

Herbert Ypma is an award-winning author, photographer, art director, traveller and entrepreneur. He has written 12 books about design and architecture including the bestselling *India Modern* and the very successful *World Design* book series. He has also written 18 books about travel including the ground-breaking *Hip Hotels* book series that sold over a million copies. Herbert Ypma is a keen surfer, sailor and skier and, like a true nomad, he divides his time between Asia, Australia, Europe and North America.

© **Bibliographical information of the Deutsche Nationalbibliothek**
The Deutsche Nationalbibliothek lists this publication in the Deutsche Nationalbibliografie; detailed bibliographical data are available on the internet at http://dnb.d-nb.de.

© Emons Verlag GmbH
All rights reserved
© Photographs by Herbert Ypma
Layout: Ralf Reiche, Weusthoff und Reiche Design, Köln, www.wundrdesign.de
Editing: Karen E. Seiger
Printing and binding: Optimal Media, Röbel/Müritz
Printed in Germany 2022
ISBN 978-3-7408-0902-7
First edition

Join us in uncovering
new places around the world at
www.111places.com

FSC
www.fsc.org

MIX
Paper | Supporting
responsible forestry
FSC® C108521